TH LETTERS Of Paul

AN INTRODUCTION TO THE APOSTLE

KEN HEMPHILL

Auxano
PRESS

Copyright ©2018 by Ken Hemphill

All Rights Reserved.

ISBN: 978-0-578-10953-4

Published by Auxano Press, Travelers Rest, South Carolina, www.AuxanoPress.com.

Cover design and Layout: CrosslinCreative.net

Cover image: LightStock.com

Printed in the United States of America

22 21 20 19 18—5 4 3 2 1

Dedication

To
Edie Banks,
my granddaughter;
a ray of sunshine, whose radiant smile
and infectious laugh brighten each day.
It was a joy to celebrate your commitment to Christ
and believer's baptism this year.
I am praying that your faith will continue to abound
as you grow in Christ.

Contents

Acknowledgments

Every book is a team effort, and those whose names do not appear on the cover of the book often deserve a great deal of the credit for the quality of the finished product.

I am grateful to the people at Auxano Press, who ensure the accuracy, beauty, and serviceability of the non-disposable curriculum that has become our signature product. I am especially indebted to Maleah Bell, who is the primary editor and project manager at Auxano Press. Her attention to detail and knowledge of the industry ensures the quality of each project. Thanks to Robin Crosslin, who designs our covers and interiors, making our material more attractive and readable. Josh Hunt assists greatly in getting our materials to Bookmasters in a timely manner. Bookmasters/Baker and Taylor prints and distributes our materials.

I have profited greatly from reading numerous excellent commentaries and books related to the topics and passages considered in this book. Because we attempt to keep footnotes to a minimum, I have only cited other works where I have quoted directly and have included supplemental materials that will help those wanting more information on the topic. My debt to others who are much better scholars than I am will be evident to many readers. I have been greatly dependent on *The New Testament: Its Background and Message* by Thomas D. Lea. I was honored to serve with Dr. Lea at Southwestern Baptist Theological Seminary.

Paula, my wife, best friend, and ministry partner of fifty years continues to be my inspiration for writing. She has endured patiently the many hours I spend in my office writing the original drafts for these books. She shares my love for the Word and the world.

My children and grandchildren are always in mind as I prepare these materials for small group Bible study. I want them to love the Lord with all their heart, soul, mind, and strength. I have been dedicating these books to my grandchildren; this is number nine in the grandkid series, and it is dedicated to Edie Banks.

Tina is our oldest, and she and her husband Brett have three children—Lois, Micah, and Naomi. Rachael and her husband Stephen have five children—Emerson, Ward, Ruby, Audrey, and Sam. Katie, the youngest, is married to Daniel, and they have four children—Aubrey, Sloane, Edie, and Shepherd. Our children and grandchildren make us proud and hopeful for the church of the future.

Finally, I want to thank Dr. Gene Fant and all my colleagues at North Greenville University, where our motto is "Christ makes the difference." It is my privilege to serve as special assistant to the president for denominational relations and as a professor in our graduate school. The development of non-disposable curricula is one facet of North Greenville's commitment to assist local churches to experience healthy, biblical growth. It is our conviction that only the Word of God applied by the Spirit of God changes the heart and mind.

Introduction

It has been my privilege to teach the New Testament to church members and students in several different settings from Southwestern Seminary to North Greenville University. They learn quickly that I love the Pauline letters. Many of my favorite verses memorized as a child came from Paul's writings. My earliest attempts at preaching as a young person would often utilize Paul's letters. I found that they virtually outlined themselves. At seminary I took many of my electives in Paul's writings. When I was privileged to study at Cambridge University, I chose a research topic that focused my study there.

As a pastor I attempted to teach from the entire Bible, believing that it is all profitable for the growth of the individual and the church. Nevertheless, I still have a special love for the Pauline letters. It stands to reason that many pastors would gravitate to these letters for informing the life and ministry of the church, since that is precisely why they were written. Each of them is an occasional letter written to a specific congregation with its own set of issues, and yet they all seem as if they were written for the issues we face today.

As I teach a survey of the New Testament, I have consistently been amused to discover that most of my students have never actually thought about the order of the letters. Some think they are in our present-day Bibles based on the order in which they were written. Truth is, they are in order based on their length, from longest to shortest. Some persons who have read or studied from a chronological Bible are aware that the chronological order of the books is quite different and that reading with this in mind often yields fruitful insights.

Each chapter of this book focuses on one of the letters, taken in its order of writing. There are minor differences among scholars about the order, but I have followed the order held by most conservative evangelical scholars. I have used two main sources in determining the date of writing—*The New Testament: Its Background and Message* by Thomas D. Lea and *The Cradle, the Cross, and the Crown* by Andreas J. Köstenberger, L. Scott Kellum, and Charles L. Quarles.

Each chapter of *The Letters of Paul* follows the same outline. After a brief introduction, we will address the matter of Paul's location and his purpose in writing. In most cases this material will come directly from the Acts narrative and the letter being studied. The second section provides an overview or an expanded outline of the letter. The final section focuses on a key passage from the letter, which will assist the reader in understanding and remembering the focus of a particular letter.

The Letters of Paul: An Introduction to the Apostle provides both a look at the apostle's life and ministry and a succinct overview of each of his letters. It is designed for small group study, but it can be used profitably by anyone who wants to gain a better understanding of Paul, his writings, the early church, and the Lord of the church.

Chapter 1

Galatians

Focal Passage: Galatians 3:1-14

Galatians has been called a letter packed with spiritual dynamite. It was the first letter written by the apostle Paul. Galatians, like all the Pauline correspondence, was an occasional letter written to a church or churches to speak to specific issues prompted by Paul's founding visit and events and misunderstandings that had occurred subsequent to his visit. As we read the Pauline letters, we need to bear in mind that we are looking at the early church in its infancy. As we might expect, these first-century Christians were often caught up in complex crosscurrents, which caused confusion and necessitated further instruction from their founder and teacher.

In writing to the Galatians, Paul found it necessary to defend his apostolic authority and understanding of the gospel, which were inextricably bound together. Therefore, the concerns that he would address were both theological and practical. Paul was intensely concerned that some persons in the Galatian churches were in danger of deserting the authentic gospel for a distorted understanding (1:6-9). He thus reminded them of their salvation experience and his ministry with them, and he explained the purpose of the law to act as a tutor to bring one to faith in Christ.

Where Was Paul? Why Did He Write Galatians?

We must pick up the story of Paul's ministry in Antioch to have a context for the first missionary journey and the letter to the

Galatians. When Barnabas arrived in Antioch and witnessed God's grace displayed in the conversion of a large number of Jews and Gentiles, he immediately left for Tarsus to bring Paul to Antioch as a ministry partner (Acts 11:25-26). Paul and Barnabas spent a year discipling the new converts. Having been told of a famine that would impact the entire world, the church sent Paul and Barnabas to Jerusalem with an offering for the relief of the believers. (vv. 29-30 [AD 46–47]).

Later, while the church was fasting and praying, the Spirit instructed them to send Paul and Barnabas to "the work to which [He had] called them" (13:2). The first missionary journey would take Paul to Cyprus and cities of Asia Minor such as Pisidian Antioch, Iconium, Lystra, and Derbe. The response was mixed, as both Jews and Gentiles believed, but some Jews strongly opposed Paul's preaching (v. 50; 14:1-2, 19). Judging from the content of Galatians, it appears that some Jewish Christians from outside the Galatian area, sometimes called Judaizers, entered these cities and taught that Gentiles who wanted to respond to the Jewish Messiah must also submit to Jewish law. This would mean that Gentile Christians would have to adopt Jewish customs and undergo circumcision (cf. 15:1).

One aspect of the strategy of Paul's opponents was to undermine his preaching by attacking the legitimacy of his apostleship (Gal. 1:13–2:10). The Gentiles' enthusiastic response to the gospel makes the issues addressed by Galatians critically important. What is necessary for one to be a Christ-follower? Must any works be added to the response of faith in Him? These issues are still critical today.

Galatians 1:2 is clear that Paul addressed this letter to the churches in Galatia, but the actual intended recipients are debated by scholars. The two possibilities are the North Galatian region, originally occupied by the Gauls, and the Roman province of Galatia (South Galatia), which included the cities of Antioch, Iconium, Lystra, and Derbe. The arguments are too long for our consideration, but the South Galatian view seems to be most consistent with the Acts account. Luke did not record a missionary journey to North Galatia.

Paul had completed his first missionary journey and had returned to Antioch where he spent "a long time" with the disciples (Acts 14:26-28). Judaizers from Judea came to Antioch teaching that circumcision was necessary for salvation (15:1). Paul and Barnabas strongly dissented, and the church sent them to Jerusalem to hear from the apostles and elders on this issue (v. 2). It is possible that Galatians was written from Jerusalem just prior to the conclusion of the Council.

So we can suggest that Paul wrote Galatians from Jerusalem in AD 49–50 to deal with the growing controversy concerning what one must do to be saved.

An Overview of the Letter

Paul's traditional greeting (Gal. 1:1-5) is more abrupt than that of most of his letters, suggesting his intense concern for the Galatian believers. He omitted his usual words of commendation and began with a defense of his preaching and a denunciation of those who were disturbing the Galatians with a false gospel (vv. 6-10).

In a second section, Paul utilized his own story of conversion and calling to defend the authenticity of the gospel he had preached that led to their conversion (1:11–2:21). He ended this section by arguing that Jews who introduced law keeping as essential to salvation were erecting a system of works they had not been able to obey (2:15-21).

The third major section is more theological in nature (3:1–5:1). Paul wanted the Galatians to understand that any attempt to rebuild a works-based salvation would contradict their own experience and that of Abraham. Further, he wanted to explain the value and purpose of the law.

The fourth section is very practical (5:2–6:10). He challenged them to stand firm and to not be subject to a yoke of slavery. They had begun the race well, but they had been hindered by the Judaizers. While the gospel grants freedom from legalism, it does not mean that believers should give in to the desires of the flesh. When believers walk by the Spirit, they will not carry out the desires of the flesh but rather produce the fruit of the Spirit. This will enable them to live productively in Christian community.

The final section (6:11-18) is a brief conclusion written by Paul in his own hand, emphasizing the authenticity of the writing and the urgency of the message. The tone is different from the conclusion of most Pauline letters, as Paul charged the Judaizers with attempting to avoid persecution that accompanied the preaching of the cross. Their goal was to gain converts for their own bragging rights, whereas Paul had determined to boast only in the cross. The marks of persecution on his body were evidence of his pure motives.

A Key Text to Consider (3:1-14)

Since this early letter was critical to establishing clearly what is required for humans to be saved, we will look at chapter 3. Paul's urgent tone makes it apparent that he was well aware of what was at stake in clarifying the simplicity of the gospel. He must defend himself and the gospel of grace. Paul contrasted faith in Christ with legalistic works as a means of salvation, establishing that the law was intended as preparation for the gospel and not a means of justification.

Introductory Questions (vv. 1-5)

One of the best ways to establish a point is to ask questions with apparent answers. Paul asked a series of six questions that cumulatively point to the work of the Spirit in the lives of the Galatian believers. The first question shows the gravity of the situation as Paul pondered who had "bewitched" them. The Galatians' response to the Judaizers was so foolish it seemed to suggest that someone had put a spell on them. The use of the word *bewitched* indicates that the Judaizers' message had created fascination and confusion in the minds of these new believers. Paul was not trying to belittle his own converts but was attempting to shock them into seeing the incongruity of their own behavior.

Paul had declared simply and clearly Christ crucified as the only means of salvation. His preaching had been like a billboard, publicly portraying the cross as God's only provision for the forgiveness of sin. A good illustration of Paul's commitment to preach the cross is in 1 Corinthians 1:18: "For the word of the cross is foolishness to those who are perishing, but to us who are being saved it is the power of God." The preaching of a crucified Messiah was a stumbling block to the Jews and foolishness to Greeks, but it was the power and wisdom of God (vv. 23-24). For the Galatians to depart from the message of the cross, which had the power to save, was foolishness.

A second simple question should suffice to show the folly of the Galatians' behavior: "Did you receive the Spirit by the works of the Law, or by hearing with faith?" (Gal. 3:2). In other words, how did your Christian life begin? Prior to their conversion experience, when they were attempting to obey the law, they had not received the Spirit. It was not until they heard the gospel and responded in faith that they received new birth through the ministry of the Spirit.

Paul continued with the logical next question: "Having begun by the Spirit, are you now being perfected by the flesh?" (v. 3). The contrast of flesh and Spirit is essentially a contrast between works and grace as it relates to salvation and consequent spiritual growth. Any and every works religion is an attempt to be justified by fleshly works. In this sense, Judaism is like other world religions. Paul would demonstrate later that it has one substantial difference in that it was intended to prepare people to hear and respond to the gospel. If one began the new life by the ministry of the Spirit, he or she must continue on to maturity by the work of the Spirit. By definition, the Christian life is supernatural from start to finish.

Two possible ways of understanding the fourth question exist, based on our translation of the Greek. Some translations say "suffer" or "endure," while others say "experience" (v. 4). Those using "suffer" or "endure" see this as referring to the persecution at the hands of the Galatians' Jewish countrymen that often accompanied a response to the gospel. If the believers returned to works of the law, the persecution they received from the Jews was unnecessary, since they had returned to the belief system of their persecutors.

Translating as "experience" may look ahead to the miracles in verse 5 and point to the wonderful spiritual experiences produced through the ministry of the Holy Spirit throughout Galatia—events such as those in Lystra where a lame man was healed (Acts 14:10). Paul could not countenance the idea that such experiences were in vain. But if the Galatians turned again to legalism, it would be as if the Spirit's ministry among them had been in vain. In either case, if the Galatians returned to works of the law it would negate the significance of the events that accompanied their salvation.

The final question serves as a summary question and brings the section to a conclusion. "So then, does He who provides you with the Spirit and works miracles among you, do it by the works of the Law, or by hearing with faith?" (Gal. 3:5). Paul once again wanted the Galatians to reflect concerning when they experienced miracles, particularly that of the new birth, and received the Spirit. It did not happen during the time they were trying to please God through works of the law but when they responded to the gospel by faith.

The Blessings of Abraham (vv. 6-9)

To fortify his case Paul moved from the Galatians' personal experience to the story of Abraham. It is likely that Paul's opponents had claimed Abrahamic lineage, insisting that it was necessary to be a child of Abraham first in order to believe in the Jewish Messiah.

The phrase "even so Abraham" in verse 6 makes it clear that the experience of the Galatians and that of Abraham were one and the same. Both had believed God, and righteousness was added to their ledger ("reckoned" to them, Gen. 15:6). Abraham recognized he was not able to receive God's promise of a son by his own effort; therefore he surrendered himself to God's word, and it was accounted to him as righteousness. Paul concluded that the true sons of Abraham are those who respond to God by faith. The phrase "who are of faith" (Gal. 3:7) was probably intended to be a direct contrast with the "party of the circumcision" (2:12). While the Judaizers boasted of their physical descent from Abraham, Paul focused on the spiritual descent of those, who like Abraham, respond to God's promises by faith.

For Paul, "Scripture, foreseeing . . . preached" meant precisely the same as God foreseeing and speaking, for what Scripture says is precisely what God says, since He was its author and directly controlled its content (3:8). God knew that the Gentiles would be justified by faith and therefore through Scripture preached the gospel beforehand to Abraham. God's way of dealing with man's sin was eternally the same for Jew and Gentile. Paul was alluding to the promise to Abraham recorded in Genesis 12:3 concerning the blessing of all nations. The sharing of "all the families of the earth" in Abraham's blessing was not based on physical kinship with Abraham and thus pointed to justification through faith. For this reason Paul referred to the promise made to Abraham as the gospel. It follows that "those who are of faith" (3:9) are blessed of God in the same way Abraham the believer was.

Redeemed from the Curse (vv. 10-14)

It seems likely that Paul may have been responding to an anticipated objection by the Judaizers. He had focused on Abraham's response of faith, but for them the critical issue was the law. They would have argued that the giving of the law to Moses was the crowning event of revelation. Therefore, even if God accepted Abraham's response of faith, it was because the law had not yet been given. Some of the rabbis actually attempted to show that the patriarchs kept the law before it was revealed.[1]

By using Scripture Paul demonstrated that righteousness cannot be established through works of law. Quite the opposite, those who seek justification through the law lie under a curse and not under blessing. Many rabbis believed that the common man of the day who had limited or no knowledge of the law was under God's curse. This is seen clearly in the statement of the Pharisees in John 7:49, "But this crowd which does not know the Law is accursed."

Paul was still contrasting between persons responding by faith and those trusting in works of the law. Surprisingly Paul asserted that those who are under the law are under a curse, a fact he supported by citing Deuteronomy 27:26. In its original context the intent was to summon Israel to confirm the words of the law "by doing them." The problem was that no one was able to fully obey the law, and thus Paul concluded that they had actually placed themselves under a curse by their own disobedience. Since the Jews knew of their own inability to obey the law, many would cling to the merits of the patriarchs, especially Abraham.

In one fell swoop Paul had dismantled any notion of being justified by works of righteousness since none obey all the law. This gives sinful humanity only two options in our approach to holy God: we can approach Him based on our own human merit (the Judaizers) or we can approach Him by faith alone (Abraham and his spiritual descendants).

Paul could not rest his case, for surely some of his opponents might still be holding to a sliver of hope that their righteous acts would be adequate before God. Paul turned again in verse 11 to Scripture for support, this time quoting Habakkuk 2:4. In its original context the issue is not faith versus works but rather faith against those with arrogant self-confidence. But isn't this precisely the issue of all who depend upon their own merit?

Paul pointed out what should have been obvious: "The Law is not of faith" (3:12). He then quoted Leviticus 18:5 to establish his point: "He who practices them shall live by them." Two fatal flaws exist in the Judaizers' position. First, if people could keep the commandments, they would still fall short of the faith requirement established by Habakkuk. Further, anyone desiring to earn merit before God through the law must actually obey all the law, which is impossible for humans. Thus Scripture actually proves that gaining righteousness by works of the law is impossible.

Since the law brings a curse on all who cannot obey it, the question remains as to how one can overcome the curse and receive the blessing promised through Abraham to the nations. Paul concluded with an emphatic note of victory: "Christ redeemed us from the curse of the Law, having become a curse for us" (3:13). For the modern-day reader the language of redemption from a curse may seem a bit strange, but the idea of redemption has clear Old Testament history. Isaiah 43:3 speaks of God giving Egypt for Israel's ransom, and a vivid picture of redemption is found in the story of Hosea purchasing his unfaithful wife (Hos. 3:2).

Humankind came under the curse of the law because of our inability to obey it. The cost of redemption from the curse is exceedingly great. Christ, who fully obeyed the law, and thus was not under the curse, became the curse for us. Paul illustrated the results of the curse by quoting Deuteronomy 21:23. Death by hanging on a tree was the visible sign in Israel of a man who was cursed by God because he had committed a sin worthy of death. Christ willingly endured a shameful death on our behalf.

As a result of Christ's self-surrender, the blessing of Abraham is now available to the Gentiles (cf. 3:8). The content of the blessing is that "we would receive the promise of the Spirit through faith" (3:14). Notice the use of "we" in the passage, which indicates that Jew and Gentile alike receive the gift of the Spirit, the clear evidence that one is a child of God. This gift is made available by Christ's atoning death but must be received through faith by both Jew and Gentile.

It is important to note that Paul concluded with a positive assessment of the law's intent. The law was added because of the transgression of humankind. Scripture shut up everyone under sin, and it kept us under its custody until faith came and thus served as a tutor to lead us to Christ (vv. 19, 22-24). Simply stated, the law demonstrates our sinful condition and our inability to obey it. This prompts us to rely fully on Christ for our release from the curse.

For Memory and Meditation

"Christ redeemed us from the curse of the Law, having become a curse for us—for it is written, 'Cursed is everyone who hangs on a tree.'" (Gal. 3:13)

---

[1] Alan Cole, *Galatians*, Tyndale New Testament Commentaries (London: The Tyndale Press, 1971), 94.

Chapter 2

1 Thessalonians

Focal Passage: 1 Thessalonians 5:12-22

Imagine that you lived in Thessalonica during the first century. You were a Gentile, but you had regularly attended the synagogue because you were attracted to the moral standards of the Jews and the teaching that Yahweh was the one true God. For several Sabbaths a visiting rabbi named Paul had demonstrated that the crucified Nazarene was the promised Messiah. You, along with many other God-fearing Greeks, some Jews, and a number of leading women had responded to Paul's message and had gathered in the home of Jason to learn more about Jesus.

One day some Jews stirred up the crowd and rallied wicked men from the marketplace to set the city in an uproar. The angry mob headed for Jason's house where Paul had been staying. Sensing the growing hostility, Jason and some of the leaders helped Paul escape to Berea before anyone was hurt. Tragically, the persecution of believers continued, and a fellow believer had died.

What questions do you think might have crossed your mind? You may have wondered about Paul's absence. Had he abandoned the church to face persecution alone? If so, could his message be trusted? You may also have had questions about some teachings upon which he wasn't able to fully expound. Wasn't the Lord supposed to return before anyone died? What would happen to the community without Paul?

Where Was Paul? Why Did He Write 1 Thessalonians?

Galatians was written from Jerusalem just before or during the Jerusalem Council, which was convened to determine whether it was necessary for Gentiles to be circumcised before they could be saved (Acts 15:2). The council celebrated the salvation of the Gentiles and decided that circumcision was unnecessary but requested that Gentile believers observe certain regulations. This request was written down, and Judas and Silas accompanied Paul and Barnabas as they returned to Antioch to deliver this good news.

After a short time, Paul and Barnabas left on a second missionary journey to encourage churches established previously. Barnabas wanted to take John Mark, but Paul refused because Mark had deserted them in Pamphylia. The disagreement ended with Barnabas taking Mark to Cyprus and Paul choosing Silas to replace Barnabas. When Paul arrived in Lystra, he recruited Timothy to join the missionary team.

Paul's steps were orchestrated by the Spirit, who forbade the mission team to go to Asia and Bithynia. When they arrived in Troas, the Lord spoke to Paul through a vision of a man inviting him to "come over to Macedonia and help us" (Acts 16:9). The missionary visited Philippi, where Lydia and her household were saved, a slave girl was delivered from an evil spirit, and Paul and Silas were imprisoned. During a midnight prayer meeting an earthquake released the prisoners who refused to leave the jail. This extraordinary action led to the conversion of the jailor and his whole household. After encouraging the believers in Philippi, the missionary team left and traveled through Amphipolis and Apollonia to reach Thessalonica.

Thessalonica was one of the most important cities in Macedonia. It was founded in 315 BC by Cassander, a general of Alexander the Great, who named the city for his wife. Its location on a protected bay in the northwest corner of the Aegean Sea led to its development as a seaport. This seaport town was a wealthy and flourishing center of trade. In Paul's day the population would have been around 200,000. The planting of a church in this significant city was critical for the continued spread of the gospel.

Paul began by teaching in the synagogue for three successive Sabbaths (Acts 17:1-9). The response was both immediate and encouraging. Some of the Jews, a large number of God-fearing Greeks, and a number of leading women joined Paul and Silas.

The Jews, jealous of Paul's success, fomented a riot by co-opting scoundrels from the marketplace. The resulting uproar turned the city into a cauldron of unrest. Looking for the missionaries, the mob attacked Jason's house, likely the place where the young church family gathered. When they discovered that Paul and Silas were nowhere to be found, they drug Jason and some of the brothers before the city officials. They angrily accused the missionaries of upsetting the world by declaring "that there is another king, Jesus" (v. 7).

The city authorities could do little to appease the angry mob since Paul and Silas had not been located. Jason and the leaders were released after the authorities received a pledge that the trouble would cease. Paul and Silas were sent to Berea after nightfall. Some of the angry Jews followed Paul there, and others continued to harass the believers remaining in Thessalonica.

In order to discredit the Christian community, Paul's detractors mounted a slander campaign against him and his ministry in Thessalonica. Paul's impassioned self-defense in 1 Thessalonians 1 through 3 suggests that their attacks may have had some measure of success. Paul's sudden disappearance and failure to return provided his detractors an opportunity to raise doubts about the preacher and his message. If Paul was a charlatan, and his message about the Christ was false, then there was no basis for the church's existence. Paul's concern was so intense that he quickly sent Timothy to strengthen the church before he wrote 1 Thessalonians.

Paul had a brief ministry in Berea and Athens (Acts 17:10-34). Silas and Timothy rejoined Paul there, but he sent them back to Macedonia to encourage the church (1 Th. 3:2). Later, they met him in Corinth (Acts 18:5) with a favorable report about the growth of the converts (1 Th. 3:6). After receiving information about the church, Paul wrote 1 Thessalonians from Corinth in AD 50 or 51.

Paul had several goals in writing the letter. First, he wanted to respond to the criticism about his motives and ministry (2:1-12). Second, he wanted to encourage believers in the face of persecution (3:1-4). Third, low moral standards in Thessalonica led Paul to explain Christian standards for morality (4:1-8). Fourth, an untimely death prompted questions about the second coming (4:13–5:11). Finally, he wrote to establish ongoing leadership for the church (5:12-22).

An Overview of the Letter
Thanksgiving for the Testimony of the Thessalonians (1:1-10)

After an initial greeting and expression of thanksgiving for the work of faith, labor of love, and steadfastness of hope demonstrated by the Thessalonians, Paul spoke glowingly of their conversion. He reminded them that they had received the word in much tribulation but with the joy of the Holy Spirit. Their response had made them an example to believers in Macedonia and in Achaia.

Paul's Defense of His Motives and Ministry (2:1-16)

Paul's absence had allowed his detractors to question his motives, behavior, and ministry. He reminded them first that opposition to the gospel was to be expected. Paul insisted that his message was free from error, impurity, and deceit. God had approved and entrusted him with the gospel, and therefore his desire was to please God, not humans. For that reason, he avoided flattery and greed.

Paul's ministry among the Thessalonians was like that of a mother gently caring for her own children and a father exhorting his children. To avoid being a burden he had provided his own support. He concluded this section by thanking God that they had been converted through the power of the Word and had been allowed to participate in the same sufferings as other authentic churches of God.

Paul's Love and Actions on Behalf of the Thessalonians (2:17–3:13)

This section gives us insight into the apostle's love for his people and describes his loving actions after his hasty departure. He wanted to return immediately but had been hindered by Satan (2:17-18). At great sacrifice Paul remained alone in Athens and sent Timothy to strengthen and encourage them (3:1-2). When Timothy returned with good news of their steadfastness and their love for Paul, it gave Paul new life (v. 8) and led to intensified prayer that he could visit them again in person. Paul prayed that their love for one another would be multiplied and that God would keep them blameless until the Lord's return (vv. 10-13).

Moral Purity and Unity (4:1-12)

Prevailing sexual laxity, prominent throughout the Roman Empire, prompted Paul to remind the Thessalonians that sexual purity is God's will (vv. 1-8). In addition to maintaining moral purity, the believers needed to deepen their love for one another (vv. 9-10). To win the respect of non-Christians they must work hard at their occupations (vv. 11-12).

Matters Related to the Lord's Return (4:13–5:11)

Someone had died since Paul's departure, which raised the question as to the believers' fate when the Lord returns. Some may have feared that death prior to the return was a punishment for sin. Paul assured them that at Christ's return the dead will rise first. They will be joined in the Lord's presence by living believers, and both will remain with Him forever (4:13-18).

Some believers desired greater specificity about the time of the Lord's return, but Paul insisted they had sufficient knowledge to behave properly and serve faithfully. The return will be unexpected, and thus believers should prepare by living disciplined, godly lives (5:4-11).

Structure for the Ongoing Life of the Church (5:12-22)

This passage provides a glimpse of the early church organized for ministry. Leaders must be appreciated and loved for the sake of the church's mission. Their role was to labor among, have charge over, and give instruction (vv. 12-13). Members were to care for one another, even those who exhibited trying behavior. All must maintain an attitude of joy by praying without ceasing, continually giving thanks, and refusing to quench the Spirit (vv. 14-19).

Concluding Comments (5:23-28)

Paul concluded with a prayer of consecration and a reminder of God's faithfulness. He requested prayer for his mission team and instructed them to have this letter read to everyone.

A Key Text to Consider (5:12-22)

Galatians 6:1-5 and our focal passage provide our earliest glimpses of the ministry structure of the early church. In them we discover several fundamental themes that will be repeated throughout the Pauline letters. First, everything in ministry is based on loving relationships. Second, some persons are gifted and called to lead. Third, all persons are called to ministry and are accountable for fulfilling their given role.

Leadership Requires Harmonious Relationships (vv. 12-13)

Paul began by requesting that church members "appreciate" and "esteem . . . very highly in love" those whom God has gifted and called into leadership functions. This may have been intended to assist Jason and the other leaders who assisted Paul while in Thessalonica and helped him escape unnoticed by authorities. In any case, for the community to survive and thrive, it was necessary for leaders to give clear direction. The book of Acts indicates that the early church planters established leaders in every church (Acts 14:23).

Little can be accomplished when relationships between church members and leaders are strained, fragile, or even hostile. Notice that the appeal to appreciate and esteem highly in love is not based on personality or personal preferences, but on "their work" (v. 13). The mission of the church is too important for us to allow our own personal agendas to hamper progress.

The mission and work of many churches have been hampered by dysfunctional relationships in the church and a lack of support for the God-called leaders. All too often we nurture suspicious attitudes that manifest themselves in a "we versus them" mentality. Loving relationships between members and their leaders is the key to peace in the church (v. 13b), and peace is essential to mission effectiveness.

Three Key Functions for Pastoral Leaders (vv. 12-13)

The Greek structure of this sentence has three present participles governed by a single article, suggesting that Paul was describing one group of persons who were to perform three specified tasks. The three tasks are not a comprehensive list of the work of the pastor or staff, but they are central to God's purpose in establishing pastoral leadership.

"Labor among you" speaks first of the rigorous labor required by one who would care for the church family. It describes the "shepherding" or pastoral care function, which is to be directed by the pastor. When Paul wrote to young Timothy, he spoke of the necessity of both physical and spiritual fitness for those called to pastoral ministry (1 Tim. 4:6-10). In verse 10 of that passage he again emphasized the hard work involved in ministry by using the two words "labor and strive."

The word "among" in verse 12 is important, because it indicates that care of the church family requires personal involvement. Laboring among the members allows the pastor to model and mentor ministry functions that will be shared by all members of the church family as verses 14-15 will make clear. It is neither possible nor biblical for the pastor to provide all pastoral care, but the pastor should participate and ensure that others are trained and encouraged in this ministry.

"Have charge over" indicates that the pastor is to exercise oversight, leadership, and protection for the congregation. "Have charge over" is modified by the phrase "in the Lord." Administrative leadership is based on spiritual authority given by God and earned through effective service. The pastor is called to be both leader and servant, requiring him to be both powerful and humble. The model of such leadership was demonstrated by the Lord, who stooped to wash feet and yet clearly led His disciples. Many churches languish because they may applaud their pastor's humble spirit, but they never allow him to provide administrative oversight.

The writer of Hebrews gives good advice in regard to our *followship*. "Obey your leaders and submit to them, for they keep watch over your souls as those who will give an account. Let them do this with joy and not with grief, for this would be unprofitable for you" (13:17). Pastors will give account to the Chief Shepherd for how they keep watch over the flock. Members are held accountable for making the task joyous and not grievous. Anything less than mutual care is "unprofitable" and will impact the ministry of the body.

"Give you instruction" in verse 12 underlines the primary task of doctrinal instruction with the purpose of making disciples. When the growth of the church in Jerusalem created a ministry challenge for the apostles, deacons were elected to enable the apostles to devote themselves to the ministry of prayer and the Word (Acts 6:4). Consistent with God's plan, the twelve were unwilling to neglect the primary role of teaching the Word. In Ephesians 4:11-16 Paul provided a vital link between gifted leaders and gifted members. The pastor/teacher must equip the saints for the work of ministry.

The question of the appropriate title and number of church leaders enumerated in the New Testament has become controversial in recent days. The New Testament is more interested in *function* than in *titles.* We have likely created titles from words that were simply descriptive of function.

Three Greek terms are found consistently in the New Testament. "Pastor" is the translation of the Greek word *poimen.* "Elder" translates the Greek *presbuteros.* "Overseer" is from the Greek *episkopos.* The three terms are used interchangeably, even in the same context, to refer to a single group of persons. For example, in Acts 20:17 Paul asked the elders from Ephesus to meet him at Miletus. He exhorted them to shepherd *(poimen)* the flock over whom God had appointed them overseers *(episkopos).* All three Greek terms are used in 1 Peter 5:1-2 to speak of the ministry of one group of persons.

My own best reading of the New Testament is that the three terms above are descriptive of the work of the pastor, who is later joined in ministry by deacons who assist with pastoral care. Rather than split hairs over titles, we need to embrace a leadership model that is biblical and productive.

The Shared Ministry of the Body (v. 14)

Paul repeated the term "brethren" in verse 14, this time using a stronger word "urge" as he focused on the responsibility for ministry that is applicable to every member of the church. The issues mentioned were specific to the needs in Thessalonica, but they establish a mandate for every member ministry.

The members were urged first to "admonish the unruly." The word "unruly" literally means "standing out of rank." We likely meet these unruly persons again in 2 Thessalonians (3:6-15).

Chapter 3

2 Thessalonians

Focal Passage: 2 Thessalonians 1:1-12

The second coming of the Lord probably elicits more interest and garners less agreement among evangelical believers than any other subject. The various views are discussed with terms such as *premillennial*, *postmillennial*, and *amillennial*. The large number of expressed opinions has made some believers declare that they are "promillennials," meaning they are "in favor of it" and others that they are "panmillennials," meaning they believe it will all "pan out" in God's good timing.

The fact that so many different views have been adopted by serious and committed believers throughout the history of the church should stand as a sentinel warning to us about being too dogmatic about our own positions. We certainly shouldn't break fellowship with those who differ with us. The nonnegotiable truth is that the Lord is sovereign over history and will return as the glorified, reigning Lord.

Paul had spoken about the second coming during his ministry in Thessalonica. Nonetheless, it is apparent that not all of his teaching had been understood by the new converts. For that reason he wrote about the second coming in his first letter, assuring believers that those who died before the Lord's return would accompany Him on His return (1 Th. 4:13-18). He argued that his readers didn't need to know anything additional about the times and epochs; they knew enough to live circumspectly in the light of His sure return (5:1-11). The first letter had not erased all confusion, and therefore Paul devoted a majority of this second letter to the topic of the second coming.

Where was Paul? Why Did He Write 2 Thessalonians?

A few persons have suggested that 2 Thessalonians was written before 1 Thessalonians, but 2 Thessalonians 2:15 seems to suggest an earlier letter existed. If we accept the traditional order, then 2 Thessalonians was written a few months after the first letter in AD 51 or 52. Paul's first letter was sent soon after his arrival in Corinth, and it seems to have solved some of the issues of concern. He had defended vigorously his personal integrity, and there is no further mention of that in the second letter.

Some believers in Thessalonica were still confused about certain issues related to the second coming, thinking the return had already occurred or was imminent. It is not clear whether this confusion was caused by a misunderstanding of Paul's oral and written instruction or whether other teachers had created unnecessary confusion. In the second letter Paul mentioned a spirit or message or letter, which had falsely been attributed to him, that the day of the Lord had already come (2:2).

This misunderstanding had prompted some persons to stop working, and they had used their idle time to meddle in the affairs of others (3:11-12). Paul had alluded to this idleness in the first letter: "Make it your ambition to lead a quiet life and attend to your own business and work with your hands, just as we commanded you" (1 Th. 4:11). Some readers were oblivious to this subtle reminder, and thus Paul had to make it crystal clear that idlers would not be supported by the community. If they persisted in their contentious behavior, the community was to withdraw fellowship with the hope that they would be brought to repentance (2 Th. 3:14-16).

Likely, the persons who bore the first letter had returned to Paul with the information that caused him to quickly pen the second letter. The tone is not adversarial, but it is stern, as we would expect from one who saw himself as an imploring father (1 Th. 2:11). Thus the letter focuses primarily on the second coming and those who have become a burden to the church by their refusal to work.

An Overview of the Letter

Thanksgiving for Their Faith and Perseverance despite Persecution (1:1-12)

After a brief introduction Paul expressed his thanksgiving for the growth of their faith and love for each other in spite of the challenges they had faced. He affirmed that he had boasted about their response to persecution to the other churches of God. Persecution would refine them, making them worthy of the kingdom of God for which they were suffering.

Paul assured them that a righteous God would bring judgment on their persecutors and provide ultimate relief to those being persecuted when the Lord Jesus is revealed from heaven with His mighty angels. They will deal out retribution to those who do not know God and refuse to obey the gospel. For those who have believed Paul's preaching, it will be a day when Christ is glorified in His saints.

Christ's Coming and the Ultimate Destruction of the Man of Lawlessness (2:1-10)

The phrase "the day of the Lord" (v. 2) is used to describe a series of events that will occur at Jesus' return. Paul encouraged the believers with the assurance that these events had not yet begun. Clearly someone had used devious means to convince some of them that the events of the end-time had begun.

Paul declared that a moral rebellion (a time of apostasy), accompanied by the appearance of a "man of lawlessness" who would exalt himself above "every so-called god or object of worship," must first occur. This man of lawlessness would demand to be worshipped as god, display "signs and false wonders," and incite all forms of evil in his followers. He works through deception, and those who follow him will face ultimate destruction because "they did not receive the love of the truth so as to be saved" (vv. 4, 9-10).

The man of lawlessness was already at work, but his display of power would increase when the restrainer was removed. In verse 6 the restrainer is spoken of using a neuter participle ("what restrains"), but in verse 7 the participle is masculine ("who now restrains"). There have been many suggestions as to the identity of the restrainer. The government, the missionary preaching of the gospel, and the Holy Spirit are among the most popular suggestions. All of these must remain in the realm of conjecture; Paul did not clarify this matter since his first-century readers knew what he was referring to.

The conclusion of the matter is what should catch our attention and give us complete assurance. "Then that lawless one will be revealed whom the Lord will slay with the breath of His mouth and bring to an end by the appearance of His coming" (v. 8). For all of his bluster and miraculous display, the lawless one is slain by the mere appearance of the one true Lord.

Gratitude and Encouragement (2:11-17)

Paul expressed thanks for God's work among the Thessalonians and encouraged them to stand firm and hold to things they had been taught in person and through the letters (v. 15). Notice the conjunction of God's choice and man's necessary response. God has chosen us from the beginning for salvation[1] when we respond to the preaching of the gospel (vv. 13-14). This is the necessary corollary to the truth that those who did not believe the truth were deluded (vv. 11-12). Paul concluded this section with a brief prayer that the believers would be comforted and strengthened for every good work.

Final Concerns and Conclusion (3:1-18)

After requesting prayer for his own gospel ministry, Paul encouraged the believers to continue in obedience (vv. 1-5). He then returned to an issue that was likely connected to the misunderstanding about the Lord's return. Some had ceased labor and had become a burden to the church. Paul thus exhorted them to avoid the habit of idleness and to earn their own way. If these idle busybodies did not obey his instructions, the church must administer discipline with the desire of ultimate restoration. He then signed the letter with his own hand and offered a final benediction (vv. 6-18).

A Key Text to Consider (1:1-12)

Second Thessalonians is a brief letter, but it is so rich I have had great difficulty deciding which passage will best assist you in understanding the purpose of this letter. I think the introductory paragraph will provide a rich study.

Greetings and Grace (1:1-2)

If you look back at the first letter, you will find that the greeting is essentially the same. A first-century letter began with the name of the writer followed by that of the addressee and an appropriate greeting. Paul followed the conventional form, but he adapted it using a Christian greeting.

Paul began by linking Silvanus and Timothy with his ministry. When Paul and Barnabas disagreed over taking John Mark on a second missionary journey, Paul chose Silvanus (also Silas) as his chief assistant (Acts 15:36-41). Silvanus was one of two men chosen to take the decision of the Jerusalem Council to Antioch and was described as one of the "leading men among the brethren" (v. 22).

Timothy was the son of a Greek father and Jewish mother. Both his grandmother and his mother were devout (2 Tim. 1:5) and had instructed him in the Scriptures from childhood (3:15). It seems that Timothy may have been somewhat timid in disposition, but Paul saw great potential in him and took him as a companion on several missionary journeys, sent him as his representative on several occasions (Acts 19:22; 1 Cor. 4:17; Phil. 2:19), and mentioned him in the greetings of six different letters (2 Corinthians, Philippians, Colossians, 1 and 2 Thessalonians, and Philemon). It is encouraging to know that God can use people of different temperaments.

The use of "God our Father" not only reminded the Thessalonians of their unique relationship with God through Jesus Christ, but it also spoke of the family bond that united them with Paul and his companions. The greeting, which combines grace and peace, may have originated with Paul. *Grace* is from the same root as the Greek word meaning "greeting." But the step from "greeting" to "grace" is significant. *Grace* means God's kindness to man, providing for his spiritual needs in Christ. *Peace* is the usual Hebrew greeting *Shalom*. For Greeks, peace essentially meant the absence of conflict, but for the Hebrew it was a positive blessing for a well-rounded life; it, too, is a gift of God.[2]

Worthy of the Kingdom of God (1:3-5)

A word of thanksgiving was common in letters of the time, but Paul adapted the form based on the need of the church. He affirmed that it would be inappropriate if he did not give thanks for them, given their response to the gospel and his teaching. He specifically mentioned his gratitude for the strengthening of their faith and the growing nature of their love for one another. We should recall that Paul had written about these two matters in the first letter (1 Th. 3:10, 12).

Because of their evident growth, Paul spoke proudly of them among the churches of God. The use of the phrase "we ourselves" in verse 4 may suggest that it was somewhat unusual for the church planter to boast about his own church. But, in this case, their perseverance and growing faith through persecutions and afflictions had caused him to broadcast this good news to all the churches. This does not mean that Paul had systematically told every church about their growth but that his praise of them had spread far and wide. It is also worthy of noting that Paul linked early churches consistently to one another as he communicated by word and letter. He was establishing an association of churches bound together by their mutual commitment to Christ.

Their "persecutions and afflictions" were a plain indication of God's righteous judgment (v. 5). We are sometimes prone to think that the suffering of Christians somehow disproves that God is working out righteous judgment. Many modern-day believers see suffering as an evil to be avoided at all costs. Yet the New Testament teaches clearly that God can and does use suffering as a means of working out His eternal purpose. For example, in Romans 5:3-5 Paul indicated that the Christian can exult in tribulation because it produces perseverance, which results in proven character, producing a hope that does not disappoint. In the Sermon on the Mount, Jesus declared, "Blessed are those who have been persecuted for the sake of righteousness, for theirs is the kingdom of heaven" (Matt. 5:10).

The Thessalonians' ability to endure and grow in faith in spite of their afflictions was a sure sign that God was working in them "so that you will be considered worthy of the kingdom of God, for which indeed you are suffering" (2 Th. 1:5). A righteous God provides all our needs, and His provision is neither haphazard nor is it impeded by suffering and affliction. The idea here is very similar to Romans 8:28-39 where Paul declared that God would work in every circumstance to conform His people to the image of His Son. He then listed a litany of things we might experience in this life, beginning with tribulation and ending with "any other created thing," and concluded with the affirmation that none can separate us from God's love (vv. 35-39).

No suggestion is given that suffering earns entry for anyone into the kingdom of God. God calls us, redeems us, gives us the grace to endure suffering, and works through suffering to make us fit for the Kingdom, "for which indeed you are suffering." Paul encouraged the church by placing their suffering in the context of the larger church and God's kingdom. Throughout the New Testament the present suffering of believers is set against the glories to come when the Kingdom comes in fullness (cf. Luke 6:21-23; Rom. 8:17; James 1:12; 1 Pet. 1:3-9; 4:12-19).

The Return of the Righteous King (vv. 6-10)

Paul then looked to the future "when the Lord Jesus will be revealed from heaven with His mighty angels in flaming fire" (v. 7). Three specific results of His return are mentioned in these verses: He will deal out retribution to those afflicting the church, give relief to the afflicted, and be glorified in His saints on that day.

God's righteous character is seen both in bringing believers to salvation and blessing in His kingdom and also in bringing judgment to those who persist in evil. This thought is begun in verse 6 and further clarified in verse 8. He will deal out "retribution" to those who do not know the Lord and "do not obey the gospel of our Lord Jesus." The word translated "retribution" is a compound based on same Greek root as the word translated "righteous" in verse 5 and "just" in verse 6. Thus, God's judgment is fully just. The basis of judgment is an individual's knowledge of God, which comes through response to the gospel of our Lord Jesus.

Leon Morris comments, "Rejection of the gospel accordingly is disobedience to a royal invitation."[3] The end result will be "eternal destruction, away from the presence of the Lord and from the glory of His power" (v. 9). The description of judgment takes one's breath away. It is eternal in duration! It will be absolute separation from the Lord and thus everything good and glorious.

In His righteousness God gives relief to the afflicted. While ultimate relief will be experienced in Christ's glorious return, the knowledge of that relief should have given hope to the Thessalonians who were going through trying times. Paul used the phrase "to us as well" (v. 6) to remind the Thessalonians that he and his companions constantly faced trials.

At His return, the Lord will be revealed in all His glory. Men might now deny His existence, but then His Lordship will be clearly seen. He will come "from heaven," accompanied by "His mighty angels," and "in flaming fire." Heaven speaks of the highest place of authority. The emphasis is on the glory and awesome power of the Lord. The "flaming fire" speaks of the majesty of His coming and reminds us of the giving of the law on Mount Sinai and the coming of the Holy Spirit at Pentecost.

Paul concluded this section by returning to the impact of the Lord's coming on those who have put their trust in Christ ("saints"). The word translated "glorified" occurs only in verses 10 and 12. Christ will be glorified "among" the saints and "in" the saints. It is overwhelming to think of the Lord's glory being reflected in us as we share it. The new age in Christ will far exceed anything we can imagine. This new glorious age will be for "all who have believed." Paul employed the aorist tense to indicate a decisive act of faith. His reference to "our testimony" emphasizes the work of the missionary team in declaring the saving truth of the gospel.

A Word of Prayer (1:11-12)

Paul was mindful that the Thessalonian believers still had to live courageously in a hard world that had brought persecution. This was a humanly impossible task, and thus Paul prayed that they would experience that strength, which only God can provide.

God alone can call humans to Himself; and at the moment of that calling, we are all unworthy. But God through His indwelling Spirit enables us to walk worthy of that calling (Eph. 4:1). The phrase "God will count you worthy" again focuses on the day when God will pronounce them worthy (v. 11; Matt. 25:21). Paul prayed that God would produce His goodness in them and that their faith would produce works that should naturally flow from faith (cf. James 2:17-18). Since this is clearly impossible in human strength, Paul ended by reminding them that this will only occur through the operation of God's power.

The ultimate goal of life is summarized in verse 12 with the phrase "so that the name of our Lord Jesus will be glorified in you." The name in biblical times summed up the character of a person (cf. Rev. 2:17). The life of every believer is a canvas upon which God wants to paint His name. The Thessalonians were to live in such a manner that their very lives would point to the one who produced His fruit in their lives. Thus, the Lord will be glorified "in you." The addition of the phrase "and you in Him" affirms that the Thessalonians would be glorified because of their relationship with Christ.

God's choosing to reveal Himself through us is beyond our comprehension. What do people see when they look at the canvas of your life?

For Memory and Meditation

"To this end also we pray for you always, that our God will count you worthy of your calling, and fulfill every desire for goodness and the work of faith with power." (2 Th. 1:11)

---

[1] For further study, see my book *Unlimited: God's Love, Atonement, and Mission* (Traveler's Rest, SC: Auxano Press, 2018).

[2] This paragraph is a summarization of Leon Morris, *The First and Second Epistles to the Thessalonians* (Grand Rapids, MI: Wm. B. Eerdmans, 1959), 49.

[3] Morris, *Thessalonians*, 205.

Chapter 4

1 Corinthians

Focal Passage: 1 Corinthians 9:1-27

Ancient Corinth was destroyed by the Roman consul Lucius Mummius in 146 BC. The site lay dormant for one hundred years until it was refounded by Julius Caesar as a Roman colony in 44 BC. The strategic location of Corinth as the sentry city of a four-and-one-half-mile isthmus that bridged the Peloponnese and the mainland and separated the Saronic and Corinthian gulfs made Corinth a strategic and desirable site.

Corinth had everything necessary to make it a prosperous and licentious city. It had a supply of good water from natural springs, a natural defense provided by the towering Acrocorinth, and two harbors, which controlled East-West commerce. It hosted the Isthmian games that ranked just below the Olympics. Corinth attracted inhabitants and guests in the way Las Vegas does today. In ancient times Corinth had a temple dedicated to the goddess Aphrodite, and worship was essentially cult prostitution. This temple was in ruins by the time Paul visited, but immorality in this seaport city was still prominent.

The Romans were dominant, and they brought their gods and culture to Corinth. But the process of Hellenization (Greek influence) had already had an impact; and since Corinth was historically Greek, it maintained its close ties with Greek religion, philosophy, and art. The religious environment was a melting pot of religious practices from East and West. Judaism, with its synagogues and belief in the one true God, was added to the religious stew. To add a pinch of spice, God tossed the apostle Paul—the greatest missionary of the first century—into the mix.

Paul established a friendship with Aquila and Priscilla, Jews from Rome who shared his profession as tentmaker and his commitment to Jesus as Messiah. Paul dedicated eighteen months to developing a Christian stronghold in this key city (Acts 18:11). The church was composed predominantly of Gentiles from the lower socioeconomic strata. Nevertheless, several wealthy families and a few leading Jews were among Paul's early converts.

Because of the success of Paul's ministry in Corinth, some Jews brought Paul before Gallio, the Roman proconsul of Achaia. The judge ruled that the accusations against Paul were nothing more than Jewish questions about words and names. This legal ruling served to legitimize Christianity in Corinth and throughout the Roman world. Paul remained in Corinth many days after this event and then left for Syria with Priscilla and Aquila (Acts 18:18). After a brief stop in Cenchrea, he came to Ephesus, where he left Priscilla and Aquila.

Where was Paul? Why Did He Write 1 Corinthians?

After Paul's departure the church at Corinth was led by Stephanas, Fortunatus, and Achaicus (1 Cor. 16:17). Other leaders must have visited Corinth during Paul's absence. Some, like Apollos, augmented Paul's message by watering where Paul had sown (3:6), but others seemed to have created confusion, particularly in regard to the meaning and appropriate use of spiritual gifts.

Meanwhile, Paul returned briefly to Antioch (Acts 18:23) and then began his third missionary journey. After passing through the Galatian region and Phrygia, Paul returned to Ephesus, where he remained for approximately three years (20:31). It is likely that this period corresponds to Apollos's ministry in Corinth (18:24-28). In God's providence, Priscilla and Aquila had met the young Alexandrian in Ephesus and had instructed him more accurately about Jesus. They encouraged him to visit Achaia and wrote to the disciples there, instructing them to welcome Apollos.

At some point after his departure from Corinth, Paul wrote a brief letter, mentioned in 1 Corinthians 5:9, that no longer exists and was misunderstood. That letter dealt with sexual immorality in the church. Later, Paul sent Timothy to deal with problems and misunderstandings (4:8-17), but his visit seems not to have been very productive. When various problems and matters of confusion continued to hamper the church's ministry, some Corinthian friends contacted Paul seeking his advice. Chloe's servants brought Paul word of disagreements that had negatively impacted fellowship in the church (1:11; 5:1).

It also seems likely that leaders in the church sent Paul a letter requesting additional information regarding several issues of doctrine and behavior. These questions and answers are indicated in the text beginning in 7:1, "Now concerning the things about which you wrote." (An abbreviated form of this formula is found in 7:25; 8:1; 12:1; 15:1; 16:1, 12). It is possible that the leaders mentioned in 1 Corinthians 16:17 may have carried this letter to Paul.

From Ephesus Paul penned a strongly worded letter we now call 1 Corinthians to deal with the reports from Chloe's people and the questions from the church family. Paul must have been near the end of his stay in Ephesus, for he was making plans to leave (16:5-8). This would mean that this letter was written around AD 55 or 56.

An Overview of the Letter

In broad strokes, the first six chapters deal with the issues that were brought to Paul's attention by Chloe's people. The response to the letter from Corinth begins with chapter seven and continues to the end of the letter.

Issues Reported to Paul (1:1–6:20)

Paul gave the traditional greeting a uniquely Christian twist and began his corrective concerning their overevaluation of their own spiritual accomplishments (1:1-9). Rather than praising their accomplishments, Paul focused on the grace of God that had been given to them (v. 4). We can hear a clear echo of their boasting in verse 5 "that in everything you were enriched in Him, in all speech and all knowledge," and in verse 7, "not lacking in any gift." Some were clearly proud of their abundance of gifts and believed them to be total and not partial, issues he would correct throughout the letter.

The first issue that had to be addressed was the factions in the church (1:10–4:21). The factions had been the result of the exaggerated loyalty to men rather than to Jesus (1:12). While we have no information that Peter had visited Rome, some knew of him by reputation and held him up against Paul. The "Christ" party probably represented a group of persons who viewed themselves as so spiritually elite that they claimed no human leader. The real issue was not related to any leader but to the spiritual immaturity of some who attached themselves to human leaders.

Paul corrected the overevaluation of human leaders by first talking about the nature of the gospel (1:18–3:4). The gospel was the message of the cross, which was foolishness to the perishing. The idea of a crucified Messiah was a contradiction to the Jews and sheer folly to the Gentiles. The people who had received the gospel actually illustrated the nature of the gospel. The world regarded them as persons who lacked influence, position, and power (1:26).

Paul provided a divine demonstration of the gospel's power by his simple preaching, which had produced the mighty results exhibited in the birth and growth of the church in Corinth (2:1-5). Further, he indicated that the gospel demonstrated true wisdom that was revealed by the Holy Spirit and produced growing maturity in believers (vv. 10-16). The fleshly behavior of the Corinthians was a clear indication that they had not yet reached maturity (3:1-4).

Paul also had to correct a false understanding of the nature of ministry. Some viewed Paul and Apollos as competitors. Paul insisted they were servants and fellow workers with God; they had simply been given different gifts and opportunities. God was the source of all growth (vv. 5-17). Human pride produced disunity, and thus Paul pointed out that it was utter folly to boast in what one had received from God (3:18–4:13). After careful reasoning about disunity in the church, Paul made a final appeal for unity, speaking of his role as their founder and father in the faith (4:14-21).

Paul had to deal with three moral issues that were impacting the church's mission. The first was a matter of an incestuous sexual relationship, which required church discipline (5:1-13). The second had to do with lawsuits among believers. Paul was grieved that believers were not wise enough to settle lawsuits among themselves (6:1-8). Finally, Paul dealt with sexual immorality in general (vv. 9-20).

Issues Raised by the Congregation (7:1–16:24)

The issues addressed in the remainder of the letter are those that were contained in the letter from the church. The first issue had to do with marriage and celibacy. In ancient times many people saw celibacy as a high calling; and while Paul admitted that celibacy was an acceptable option for those so gifted, marriage was the norm. While he gave specific counsel to those widowed or divorced, his basic teaching was for all to live contentedly in the state where they found themselves (7:1-40).

The issue of meat offered to idols is dealt with in the next three chapters (8:1–11:1). The issues were complex. Pagan shrines, which received sacrifices for their gods, supplied meat for the market. Should a Christian buy such meat? At other times Christians might be invited to eat meat in a private home where idol meat from the market might be served. It was also possible that a Christian might be invited to attend services, such as a wedding celebration, in a pagan temple.

Paul offered at least three key limitations to one's freedom in these matters. First, everything possible should be done to avoid offending a weaker brother. Second, freedom should be limited if the action might hinder the spread of the gospel. Finally, individuals should not indulge in any activity that threatened their own spiritual lives (8:9; 9:12; 10:6-14).

The next major section is related to public worship (11:2-34) and the disunity created by those who wanted to demand their own rights. The women have the right to pray and prophesy if they do so with appropriate decorum and with the desire to edify (vv. 5-16). A second issue relates to the Lord's Supper, which was taken as a part of a fellowship meal. The wealthy ate to excess while the poor went hungry. Their practice established factions and thus was not truly the Lord's Supper. Paul counseled them to focus on the meaning of the death of Christ and His imminent return (vv. 20-34).

The longest section (12:1–14:40) deals with the proper use of spiritual gifts. In chapter 12 Paul broadened the understanding of spiritual gifts by using the image of the diverse human body. In a second gift list he added leadership gifts and mundane service abilities. Paul established that gifts do not demonstrate advanced spirituality and acknowledged that love or the fruit of the Spirit is the sign of spiritual maturity and that which provides control for the seeking and utilization of all gifts (ch. 13). In chapter 14 he gave directions for how the mature believer seeks and uses gifts for the edification of the body.

Chapter 15 is a powerful chapter on the resurrection. Paul established its historical credibility by listing numerous eyewitnesses, declaring that many were still alive. He pondered the question of what would be the consequences if the resurrection had never occurred and then concluded with the grand affirmation of the resurrection and the surpassing glory of the resurrection body. The teaching on the resurrection and return of the Lord ends with a call to steadfast service.

In the final chapter Paul gave specific directions for the offering of the saints in Jerusalem. He instructed the Corinthians about his own plans and the plans for the offering. He gave final instructions about the visit of Timothy and Apollos and the ministry of the men he had left in charge when he left Corinth.[1]

A Key Text to Consider (9:1-27)

Many persons in Corinth were enamored with their spiritual rights and the freedom from the law the gospel offered. They boasted about their advanced knowledge and then based their behavior on that "supposed" knowledge. In chapters 8 and 9 Paul discussed two issues that may seem unrelated. The first had to do with eating meat offered to idols, and the second was Paul's right as an apostle to receive pay for his ministry. But the illustration of Paul's willingness to forego his right as an apostle is a key to understanding much of this letter. A common theme throughout is the willingness of the mature believer to give up a right if his or her actions would prove harmful to a weaker brother, harm the fellowship of the church, or impact the spread of the gospel.

Take a Lesson from Paul (vv. 1-14)

Paul used his own ministry in Corinth as an example of one who willingly gave up his rights for the sake of the gospel. At the same time, this allowed Paul to address some of the issues his detractors had raised against his ministry. Some had attacked his apostolic legitimacy because of his unwillingness to take compensation for his work.

This section begins with a series of rhetorical questions that all anticipate a positive response. Paul's first question is a general one concerning the liberty of all believers, clearly linking this section with the preceding discussion. He followed the first question with a more specific one that deals with the authority and rights of an apostle. His two follow-up questions indicate that some in Corinth questioned his apostolic authority. Paul had not been one of the original eyewitnesses, but his witness to the resurrected Christ on the Damascus road was well-known. The use of "Jesus" without the word "Christ" is rare for Paul and was probably intended to place an emphasis on the human nature of Jesus, who appeared to him on the Damascus road.

A further testimony to Paul's legitimacy as an apostle was the very existence of the church in Corinth. They were the seal of his apostleship (v. 2). A seal was both a mark of ownership and a means of authentication in ancient days. These two affirmations were Paul's defense to any who wanted to examine his apostolic credentials (v. 3).

The rhetorical questions that follow represent the rights properly accorded to an apostle. The first speaks to the apostle's right to anticipate that the church would provide for his maintenance (v. 4). The second speaks of the right of an apostle to bring his wife with him and have her needs cared for (v. 5). He illustrated by referring to Cephas and the Lord's brothers. "The brothers of the Lord" is likely a reference to the children of Joseph and Mary (e.g., James and Jude). He then asked if he and Barnabas had been excluded from the right to earn one's living from ministry (v. 6).

In verse 7 Paul used three different examples to indicate that it is quite natural that workers will be fed by means of their occupation. No soldier serves at his own expense. The owner of the vineyard eats the fruit from the vineyard, and the shepherd consumes some of the milk from the flock. Paul quoted from Deuteronomy 25:4, which prohibits the muzzling of an ox while he is threshing. He concluded with the rhetorical question, "God is not concerned about oxen is He?" This passage was speaking figuratively about human needs, and therefore it is fair to conclude that God's design was for one to be fed (paid) by one's ministry (vv. 8-9).

Paul answered the question of verse 9 with another in verse 10 and then gave a clarion answer. Both the one who plows the field and the one who gathers the crop should share equally in the harvest. The language here is reminiscent of 3:6-7 where Paul spoke of his role in planting and Apollos as the one who watered. Paul's point was clear: "If we sowed spiritual things in you, is it too much if we reap material things from you?" (9:11).

As the founder of the church, Paul should have expected compensation from the Corinthians. The entire argument turns with the use of the term "nevertheless" in verse 12. Paul preferred to give up his right to their support "so that we will cause no hindrance to the gospel of Christ."

The contrast between Paul and the arrogant Corinthians could not be more striking. They insisted on their right to eat idol meat even if it meant offending a weak brother. Later, in chapter 14, the silence of certain gifts will be based on the same principle of the willingness to give up one's rights for the edification of others. Those who thought they were "strong" were actually the "weak" whom Paul took into account in his decision not to take support from the Corinthian church (cf. 2 Cor. 7:11-15).

Paul concluded with one final example from the Old Testament to fortify his case that those who proclaim the gospel should get their living from it (vv. 13-14). The priests who served at the altar were allowed to eat a portion of the food offered on the altar (Lev. 7).

All Things for the Sake of the Gospel (vv. 15-23)

Paul was not establishing his claim to future support. He was tenacious about his conviction and declared that he would rather die than for his present arrangement to be altered (v. 15). The compulsion to preach the gospel provided no basis for boasting. Paul could not imagine not preaching the gospel and saw some undefined calamity or punishment if he failed to discharge his duty (v. 16).

Paul was compelled to preach, and if he did so with a willing spirit he merited a reward. Even if he were to preach against his will, he still must do so, because it was a stewardship entrusted to him (v. 17). Paul had to preach, but he did not have to preach without compensation. The privilege of preaching without pay was his reward. It enabled him to make full use of his rights in the gospel, which became an example for the Corinthians (v. 18).

Paul was a Roman citizen and thus a free man, but he chose to be a servant that he might win more to Christ (v. 19). The idea of winning the lost permeates this entire section. In verse 20 it is those "who are under the Law"; in verse 21 it is those who are "without law"; and in verse 22 it is to "save some."

To the Jews Paul became as a Jew. He would not unnecessarily antagonize his own people because his desire was to win them to faith in Christ. "Those who are without law" is a reference to Gentiles. In reaching Gentiles, Paul did not try to bind them to all the Jewish regulations. He was not without restraint or boundaries, and therefore he indicated that he was "under the law of Christ."

You can hear Paul's passionate concern for the lost in his affirmation, "I have become all things to all men, so that I may by all means save some" (v. 22). Paul's conduct was determined by the gospel, and thus he looked forward to sharing in the blessings of salvation along with those he was privileged to reach through his preaching (v. 23).

The idea of becoming all things to all men does not mean we should live like a chameleon and disavow our own principles. Paul was unwilling to compromise when it came to the core values and the nature of the gospel. However, when no issue of principle was at stake, he was willing to conform to practices that would enable him to reach people in their unique context.

Living with Purpose (vv. 24-27)

Paul concluded the section with powerful athletic imagery. A race yields only one winner, and the Christian should put forth maximum effort to live victoriously (v. 24). Each contestant in the Isthmian games had to undergo strict training and exercise self-control to qualify to compete. These competitors were living disciplined lives to win a perishable pine wreath. The Christian, however, has in sight an imperishable crown (v. 25).

In verses 26-27 Paul mentioned first a runner losing sight of the finish line, and thus losing a race, and a boxer wasting energy beating the air. The boxer could be shadowboxing or swinging but missing an opponent. Paul disciplined his body, making it his slave, so that he would not be disqualified in the one race that mattered. He did not fear that he might lose his salvation but that he might forfeit his crown by failing to accomplish the purpose for which God had created and gifted him.

These images of the self-denial of an athlete who competes for a perishable reward is a stinging rebuke to halfhearted and undisciplined Christian service. To win many to Christ, we must avoid sin and joyfully put aside anything that hinders our total effectiveness.

For Memory and Meditation

"I do all things for the sake of the gospel, so that I may become a fellow partaker of it." (1 Cor. 9:23)

---

[1] For a full study of 1 Corinthians, see my book *Living from Grace to Glory* (Traveler's Rest, SC: Auxano Press, 2017).

Chapter 5

2 Corinthians

Focal Passage: 8:1-15

We have already had the opportunity to look at Paul's first letter to the Corinthians. The content of that letter was guided by reports Paul had received about the community and questions posed to him through a letter. Both Corinthian letters are complex because this was certainly a complex community. Many of the issues can be explained by an immature enthusiasm for certain visible and audible gifts and their impact upon others in the church.

Paul used the word *spirituals* frequently to refer to a certain group of persons who were zealous for certain gifts that they believed to demonstrate their spiritual ascendancy. Paul's primary correctives are best expressed by the two words *grace* and *love*. The understanding of the grace of all life would put an end to all boasting about gifts and gifted leaders. Love would put an end to all division and inappropriate use of gifts. Love would mandate that one desire the gifts that would most readily edify the church and use all gifts in a manner that would promote edification and evangelism. Several issues were not fully resolved by Paul's first letter, so it was necessary to write again.

Where Was Paul? Why Did He Write 2 Corinthians?

In the last chapter of 1 Corinthians (16:5-10) Paul shared his plans to come again to Corinth after he traveled through Macedonia. This would allow him to spend the winter of AD 55–56 with the

Corinthians. He explained that it was necessary for him to remain in Ephesus until Pentecost, because a wide door for effective ministry had been opened to him, even though he had experienced much opposition. He explained that it was possible that he might be able to send Timothy to visit Corinth in his absence. If such a visit proved possible, the Corinthians were to treat Timothy with due respect and send him on his way in peace.

Paul's plans were quickly modified, and he decided it would be necessary to visit Corinth both on his way to Macedonia and on his return from there. After the second of these two visits, he would set sail for Palestine to deliver the collection for the saints in Jerusalem (cf. 2 Cor. 1:15-16). Once again, Paul found it impossible to carry out this modified plan because of "our affliction which came to us in Asia" (2 Cor. 1:8). We don't know the details of the affliction, but we do know that Paul feared for his life (v. 9). A second issue that led to the modification of his plans was the news of further trouble in Corinth, which called for an urgent visit.

Apparently, Timothy had not been sufficiently bold to enforce Paul's instructions. Possibly Timothy brought back discouraging news that convinced Paul that a confrontational visit would be necessary to resolve the tension and quell a rebellion against him in Corinth. During a brief second visit Paul warned them to deal with the persons who were demanding proof that Christ was speaking through him (13:2-3). It was painful and humiliating for Paul and his converts (2:1). After that visit Paul apparently fulfilled his plans to "go through Macedonia" (1 Cor. 16:5).

Paul then sent a letter written "out of much affliction and anguish of heart" (2 Cor. 2:4). The intent was not to hurt anyone but to assure them of the love he had for them. The letter, sent by the hand of Titus, called on them to reaffirm their love for Paul and discipline those leading the opposition. This "tearful letter" has not been preserved, and thus we can only hint at its reconstruction. Paul met Titus in Macedonia and received the good news that the letter had been effective and that the Corinthians had renewed their love and loyalty to Paul (7:5-9). Paul immediately sent the letter we call 2 Corinthians. This would mean that we can date the letter to AD 56 or 57.

An Overview of the Letter

The preface (1:1-11) contains a brief greeting that follows the general form of a salutation of a letter from this period. Further, Paul expressed thanksgiving for the encouragement and protection he had received (vv. 3-11).

Addressing the Issue of the Opponents (1:12–7:16)

The first major section focuses on the issue of Paul's opponents in Corinth. Paul answered some of the attacks directed against him related to his travel plans and his motives in ministry. His alteration of travel plans had been based on his desire to avoid an unpleasant encounter. Some of Paul's opponents had attacked his character, and thus he began with a general defense of his integrity. He realized that if his opponents attacked his character it could actually have a negative impact on the message he preached and the faith of the Corinthians. He thus affirmed that his relationships and ministry were motivated by holiness and sincerity (1:12–2:4).

Likely, the missing severe letter recommended that the church discipline the leader of those who were opposing Paul. The church had followed Paul's directions, and the offender had been overwhelmed with sorrow. Thus, Paul encouraged the church to reaffirm their love for the offender (2:5-8). Paul was greatly encouraged to hear that the church stood with him, and he declared that the very existence of the church at Corinth was the affirmation of his apostolic ministry. Paul affirmed that any ministry in the Spirit was superior to that of Moses and that any afflictions he might experience were insignificant in light of the glory being stored up for him (3:12–4:18).

A particularly important passage is 5:11–7:4, where Paul talked about the ministry of reconciliation that had been given to him, and by implication, to all believers. Christ's love compels believers to become ambassadors, urging people to be reconciled to God. Such a lofty view of ministry compels believers to endure hardships and purify ourselves from any impurity.

Completing the Collection (8:1–9:15)

The second section of the letter focuses on the collection for the Jerusalem Christians who had been impoverished by a famine. This was a grand offering that involved the churches of Achaia and Macedonia. This offering, first mentioned in Acts 11:27-30, was a passionate concern for Paul because it met the needs of the saints, authenticated his Gentile mission, and gave glory to God. We will look at this section in greater detail as part of the key text.

A Strong Defense of Paul's Apostolic Authority (10:1–13:14)

The final section begins with a marked change in tone, suggesting some persons had ignored the warnings of the severe letter or that additional rebellion had occurred. We must assume that Paul heard about this after he had written the first nine chapters.

Paul was forced once again to speak strongly in defense of his apostolic authority and missionary practices. He would speak only of the work the Lord had accomplished through him and would not commend his own work. Paul's opponents were deceitful and claimed for themselves a deeper knowledge of God's plans and workings. They gladly took money from the gullible Corinthians, whereas Paul refused because of their immaturity and the boasting of the false teachers.

The section from 11:16 to 12:13 is sometimes referred to as Paul's "fool's speech." His opponents had boasted in their visions and revelations to give authority to their teaching. Paul cited his own ecstatic experiences but quickly indicated his preference to boast in his weaknesses and hardships. It was through his weaknesses that God's power was most clearly manifest.

Paul concluded by assuring the Corinthians that his motives were pure and that his only desire was their edification. He spoke of a third visit in which he would not spare any offenders who did not repent, and he challenged his readers to examine themselves to make sure their faith was sure. His concluding exhortation is a call to unity and peace. Notice also that his benediction contains a clear Trinitarian formula: "The grace of the Lord Jesus Christ, and the love of God, and the fellowship of the Holy Spirit, be with you all" (13:14).

A Key Text to Consider (8:1-15)

Paul was in Antioch when he first heard of the famine that was ravaging the believers in Jerusalem. The church in Antioch responded immediately by sending an offering to Jerusalem by Barnabas and Saul (Acts 11:27-30). The great Apostle to the Gentiles was so moved by the need of the Jerusalem Christians that he devoted the decade of the 50s to collecting an offering for the Jewish believers.

Corinth was one of the churches Paul encouraged to support this cooperative offering. He made the appeal in person first and then wrote about the need to set aside money weekly on the first day of the week. Their giving was to be proportionate based on the resources they had been given (1 Cor. 16:1-4). Now, nearly a year later, Paul had to encourage them to conclude the collection. In this context Paul shared several timeless principles of generous giving that encourage and challenge Christians in every generation.

The Grace of Giving (8:1-7)

In the first seven verses, Paul repeated the word *grace* four times. We need to recall that the early church had inherited the principle of tithing (10 percent) and the giving of alms from the Jewish community. Jesus clearly anticipated that His followers would practice both (cf. Matt. 6:1-4; 23:23), but He stressed the importance of avoiding ostentation and self-righteousness in one's giving. In other words, Jesus taught that giving is a privilege that flows naturally from the understanding of the graciousness of all of life.

Paul articulated clearly the theme of grace as he related to the Corinthians the story of the gracious giving of the churches in Macedonia—Philippi, Thessalonica, and Berea. Paul actually used the term "grace" in the context of giving in 1 Corinthians 16:3 where he referred to the offering the Corinthians were collecting as a gift. *Generosity* is a visible expression of *grace received*! Only the Holy Spirit can motivate people to give generously and spontaneously to people they have never seen. Only the Holy Spirit can enable people to give beyond their natural ability.

The Macedonian churches provided a great example of grace giving because they gave despite "a severe trial brought about by affliction" and their "extreme poverty" (2 Cor. 8:2 CSB). In spite of poverty their "abundance of joy" had "overflowed in a wealth of generosity." Joy and generosity are twins. Joy comes from the knowledge of grace received and sins forgiven. The infinite generosity of God experienced in our redemption, when truly comprehended, will produce a life of joyful giving. Joy leads to generosity, and generosity, in turn, gives one joy. *Generosity* indicates giving that is uncalculating and unpretentious, free from human motivation and pride. *Miserly people are miserable, and generous people are joyous.*

The word *grace* actually means "generosity"; the generosity of God freely gives sinners the forgiveness they don't deserve and could never afford. The use of "grace" in relation to giving doesn't simply mean it was motivated by grace; it actually suggests that giving is an act of grace. It is inspired and empowered by the Holy Spirit.

If you have read 1 Corinthians, you know that the Corinthians were "zealous" for "spiritual gifts." Their hunger to possess the more spectacular gifts was often motivated by the desire to be known as "spiritual persons." Paul attempted to redirect their zeal by encouraging them to seek those gifts that would edify the church (1 Cor. 14:12). Now, Paul was affirming that the ability to give generously "beyond their ability" is as much a demonstration of the Spirit's work as is prophecy or miracle-working faith.

You may be wondering what distinguishes "grace giving" from other forms of giving. We find here five unique characteristics.

1. Grace giving is spontaneous. The phrase "of their own accord" indicates that no one coerced them into giving. In the light of their poverty, it is possible that Paul was reluctant to mention the offering to them. Their desire to give was so overwhelming;

they were "begging us with much urging" (2 Cor. 8:3-4). Grace givers see giving as privilege, not duty.

2. Grace giving goes beyond one's natural ability. Paul indicated that they gave "according to their ability, and beyond their ability" (v. 3).

3. Grace giving enables us to move beyond *proportionate giving* (1 Cor. 16:2) to *supernatural giving.* Some who argue that the tithe (10 percent) is Old Testament legalism are often looking for an excuse to give less. Those who have experienced grace should desire to give more. If tithing could be accomplished by the Jews without the Spirit, how should the Spirit-filled believer respond?

4. Grace giving sees giving as an opportunity to share in ministry. Despite their affliction and poverty, the Macedonian believers would not be deprived of the "favor of participation in the support of the saints" (2 Cor. 8:4). Paul utilized numerous words to describe this offering. The word translated "favor" is the word *charis*, usually translated "grace." The second word is *koinonia*, often translated "fellowship" (cf. 1 Cor. 1:9; Gal. 2:9). The word translated "support" (or "ministry" CSB) is *diakonia* from which we derive the English word "deacon." Giving is a ministry of fellowship empowered by grace.

5. Grace giving begins with the gift of oneself. The Macedonians "gave themselves to the Lord and to us by the will of God" (8:5). All giving stems from offering ourselves to the Lord as a living sacrifice (Rom. 12:1). When that transaction occurs, we naturally look for opportunities of gracious service.

Paul was so encouraged by the generosity of the Macedonians he urged Titus to return to Corinth, "so he would also complete in you this gracious work as well" (8:6). In verse 7 Paul moved beyond an appeal based on the example of the Macedonian churches by reminding the Corinthians of the spiritual riches God had made available to them. This verse is reminiscent of 1 Corinthians 1:4-5 where Paul speaks of the abundance of their spiritual gifts. Paul used the pride in spiritual gifts to motivate them to "abound in this gracious work also." Generosity is evidence of grace and thus a work of the Spirit.

Love: the Supreme Motive for Giving (vv. 8-15)

Paul refused to appeal to his apostolic authority to exert any pressure that would "guilt" them into giving. He wanted their giving to be motivated by love so they would receive the full blessing that comes from joyful giving. Their generous giving would indicate "the sincerity of your love also" (v. 8). It is fascinating to notice that love begins and ends this entire section (cf. v. 24).

Paul appealed next to Christ as the supreme example of one who gave as an expression of love: "For you know the grace of our Lord Jesus Christ, that though He was rich, yet for your sake He became poor, so that you through His poverty might become rich" (v. 9). "Became poor" translates an aorist verb indicating Paul wanted the Corinthians to think of the Incarnation. Before He became man, Christ shared fully in the Father's glory (cf. John 17:5) and thus was infinitely rich. Christ laid aside the riches of glory to become a suffering servant (Phil. 2:6-7).

When one fully comprehends God's gift of infinite love, a command to give should never be necessary. Paul gave his opinion, declaring that the completion of the offering "is to your advantage" (8:10). Their giving would not only relieve the suffering of the saints in Jerusalem, but it would also allow them to demonstrate the genuineness of their love and further open them to the fullness of God's blessing. Their zeal to begin the offering must be matched by their zeal to complete it. Once one is prepared to give, God will provide the necessary resources (v. 12).

Verses 13-15, with their concluding appeal to the story of the miraculous provision of manna in the wilderness, may have been prompted by the criticism of the offering on the premise that relief for the poor could prove a hardship on givers in Corinth. Paul dismissed such a baseless excuse by asserting that such thinking is based on a lack of understanding of the resources God is prepared to make available.

Like the miraculous manna, there will be neither too much nor too little. The goal of sacrificial giving is not luxury for one and poverty for another, but equality. Equality is not to be understood in terms of socialism, which takes from the rich and redistributes to the poor, but in terms of mutual sharing that exists in a healthy family system. At the time of this letter, the surplus available to persons in Corinth could help solve the problem of need that existed in Jerusalem. In the course of time, it might be possible that the Jerusalem church would be able to meet a need of those in Corinth. Even if that never occurred, the Corinthians would surely profit from the prayers of those blessed by their generosity (9:14).

Epilogue

Paul gave detailed instructions for the administration of the offering (8:16-24). Generous giving requires that any offering be handled in such a manner that it instills trust and glorifies the Lord. Paul told the Corinthians who would be responsible for taking the offering to Jerusalem (vv. 16-19). When givers reflect the generosity of the Lord, it is critical that the offering be handled in such a way that glory continues to be reflected upon the Lord. I love verse 21: "For we have regard for what is honorable, not only in the sight of the Lord, but also in the sight of men."

According to Romans 15:25-27, the offering was completed successfully, and the great apostle was able to accompany the delegation who delivered the love offering to the needy saints in Jerusalem. "Yes they were pleased to do so, and they are indebted to them. For if the Gentiles have shared in their spiritual things, they are indebted to minister to them also in material things" (v. 27).

For Memory and Meditation

"For you know the grace of the Lord Jesus Christ, that though He was rich, yet for your sake He became poor, so that you through His poverty might become rich." (2 Cor. 8:9)

Chapter 6

Romans

Focal Passage: Romans 12:1-21

Rome, a small village on the Tiber River founded in 753 BC, had grown into a powerful metropolis of more than one million people. The many successes of Roman military leaders had brought great wealth to the city. People from numerous ethnic backgrounds walked the streets of Rome and freely practiced their diverse religions.

We can only speculate about the founding of the church in Rome. Paul's statements in 1:13 and 15:23 indicate that he was not involved in the church's founding. We can suggest that the church was founded by Jews and proselytes from Rome who had been converted through the events surrounding Pentecost. They carried the gospel back to Rome after their conversion in Jerusalem. Paul's statement that he had long desired to come to Rome (15:23) indicates that the church had existed for a reasonable period prior to the writing of this letter. The listing of several names in Romans 16 suggests that numerous house churches existed.

The expulsion of the Jews from Rome under Emperor Claudius in AD 49–50 may indicate that the church was well established by that date. Suetonius, a Roman historian, indicated that the expulsion was the result of unrest caused by "Chrestus." Many believe that "Chrestus" is a corrupted spelling for "Christus," or Christ. The expulsion of Jewish Christians would also explain the presence of Aquila and Priscilla in Corinth and other Roman

Christians that Paul may have encountered during his travels (cf. Rom. 16). Further, it explains why the news of the vitality of Christianity in Rome was proclaimed throughout the whole world (1:8).

Where Was Paul? Why Did He Write Romans?

Clues for the writing of the Roman letter are contained in the letter itself. Take a quick look at Romans 15:23-29 for our first clue. Paul dedicated much of the decade of the AD 50s to the collection of an offering, mentioned first in Acts 11:27-30, for the saints in Jerusalem because of a famine there. The initial offering was provided immediately by the disciples in Antioch, who sent it by Paul and Barnabas to the elders in Jerusalem.

Paul continued to encourage the churches of Macedonia and Achaia to give generously to this offering. In 1 Corinthians 16:1-4 Paul mentioned that the instructions being written to the Corinthians were the same as those he had previously given to the churches of Galatia. Upon his return to Corinth he would send their chosen delegates to carry the gift to Jerusalem.

Paul's return to Corinth was unexpectedly delayed, so in 2 Corinthians Paul reminded the believers there to complete the offering. He spoke of the generosity shown by the Macedonian churches, who gave in spite of the great affliction they had experienced (8:1-6).

According to Romans 15, this offering had been completed, and Paul was on his way to Jerusalem to deliver it. This love offering from the churches of Macedonia and Achaia would assist the saints in Jerusalem, and it would give credence to Paul's ministry to the Gentiles. Since the Gentiles had shared in spiritual things that came through the Jews, it was appropriate for them to minister to the Jews in terms of material things (v. 27).

This sequence of events would indicate that Paul wrote Romans after 2 Corinthians, since the collection of the offering was not yet complete when Paul dispatched that letter. He most likely wrote Romans during the three months he spent in Greece (likely Corinth) on his third missionary journey (Acts 20:3), making the date somewhere between AD 55 and 57. The three months he spent in the home of Gaius (Rom. 16:23) provided sufficient time and opportunity for the composition of such an extensive and well-organized treatise.

Paul's reasons for writing are stated well in the letter itself:

1. In the first chapter (vv. 10-15) he indicated that he had longed to see them so that he might impart some spiritual gift to them and that they would be mutually encouraged, each by the faith of the other.

2. He saw the visit as an opportunity to preach the gospel and obtain some evangelistic fruit in Rome (v. 13).

3. After delivering the offering to the poor in Jerusalem, Paul planned to travel through Rome as he journeyed to Spain in his missionary travels. He desired for the Roman church to assist him in his effort to take the gospel to the known world (15:24).

4. Paul was aware of some issues that were causing concern and disunity in the church. He wanted to help them to resolve these (chs. 12–15).

An Overview of the Letter

Various commentators have suggested different themes for the main thrust of Romans, suggesting that this letter does not have a single predominant theme. Great theological themes such as justification by faith, union with Christ, and the history of salvation are found in chapters 1–11. Practical matters such as gifted ministry, the believer's responsibility to secular government, and Christian unity are discussed in chapters 12–16.

In his salutation (1:1-17) Paul followed the standard letter format but gave it a distinctively Christian emphasis. At the end of the introductory section Paul introduced the righteousness of God as one major theme of the letter.

The Sinfulness of All Persons (1:18–3:20)

It was necessary for a righteous God to reveal wrath against sinners because they were living in moral disobedience and rebellion. Paul provided convincing evidence that men and women are all transgressors. He began with the Gentiles, charging that they had willfully rejected the truth. Their deliberate ignorance led to gross immorality, and God gave them over to their own sinfulness.

In a surprising turn, Paul emphasized that Jews were equally guilty before God and practiced the same vices they condemned in others (2:1-24). He redefined what it meant to be truly Jewish. Rather than a physical relationship to Abraham and outward circumcision, it was inner circumcision of the heart that issued a right spiritual relationship with God. Paul concluded his argument with a collection of verses, largely from the Psalms, proving that all human beings are sinful (3:9-20) and in need of redemption.

The Path of Righteousness (3:21–5:21)

Paul then focused on God's plan to deal with man's sin and provide His righteousness to humanity. True righteousness is apart from the law, founded on faith in Jesus Christ, and made available to all through His atoning death (vv. 21-26). Paul used the word "justified" to describe the divine act by which God declares as righteous anyone who places his or her trust in Jesus Christ, providing a new standing before God and the basis and incentive for holy living.

Paul referred to Abraham and David to illustrate the principle of justification by faith (4:1-25), arguing that Abraham believed in God's promise (Gen. 15:1-6) and that David was pardoned by casting himself on God's mercy (Ps. 32:1-2).

Then he presented a list of blessings for those who experience justification (5:1-11). Paul concluded with a contrast between Adam and Christ. Adam was the head of humanity whereas Christ is the head of new redeemed humanity. The relationship of sin and death in Adam had been broken and was replaced by grace and life in Christ. The law caused sin to increase, but the experience of grace removed the reign of sin and death, providing eternal life through Jesus Christ our Lord (vv. 20-21).

The Path of Holy Living (6:1–8:39)

Paul anticipated that someone might argue that the teaching of grace would cause persons to sin more to receive more grace. His initial response was "May it never be!" (6:2). He further explained that salvation results in persons receiving a new nature that delights in serving God (vv. 3-14).

Paul continued his argument for holy living with an analogy from marriage. Just as death terminates marriage, death of the believer with Christ gives the believer the freedom to enter into union with Him, producing freedom to serve by the Spirit (7:1-6). The presence of the law actually stimulates an awareness of and desire for sin (vv. 7-13). While all believers are dragged toward disobedience by the power of sin through the flesh (vv. 14-25), there is a path to victory when the believer is controlled by the Spirit of God (8:1-4).

The present experience of the Spirit and the assurance of the future resurrection are the twin pillars that help believers live patiently and victoriously in the trials of the present (8:18-30). The potential of present victory and future assurance caused Paul to burst into praise and worship (vv. 31-39).

The Problem of Israel's Unbelief (9:1–11:36)

This section was passionately personal for Paul, as the first verses indicate. How was it possible for God's own people and Paul's kindred to reject the gospel that originated with them? They were the chosen people; and the law, the covenants, the temple, the patriarchs, and the Lord Himself had come from among them (9:1-5).

Because of the failure to focus on the total context, this section of Scripture is frequently misinterpreted. These passages vividly illustrate Romans 8:28, and they demonstrate that God is greater than evil and thus at work in everything for good to those who love Him. In chapters 9 and 10 Paul grieved over the stubborn unbelief of his kinsmen (9:1-3; 10:21). Then in chapter 11 Paul affirmed that sovereign God was at work for good through the rejection of Jesus by the Jews, opening a door of salvation for the Gentiles. He further anticipated that salvation of the Gentiles might create a jealous hunger for Christ among the Jews, leading to their salvation as well (vv. 11-12).

Paul emphasized that the atonement is available to all who call upon Him (10:12). The conclusion of the section in 11:32 is critical for understanding the thrust of the entire section. "For

God has shut up all in disobedience so that He may show mercy to all." He ended by reflecting on the riches of God's wisdom and knowledge. If the Jews' rejection of the Messiah resulted in the expansion of the gospel to the Gentiles, it would ultimately bring greater glory to God. Paul believed that all persons are capable of responding to the gospel, and this truth motivated him to engage in a global mission (10:14-21).

Practical Christian Living (12:1–15:13)

In this section the theological truths of the first eleven chapters are applied, making it clear that orthodox teaching should result in holy living. Based on the mercies of God, all believers are to make themselves available to God and use wisely the gifts God has given them. These gifts are used in the context of community, which requires the manifestation of love (12:1-21).

In regard to secular authorities, the Christian is to practice respect and pay taxes (13:1-7). Believers owe love to everyone (vv. 8-10) and thus should live in a state of moral watchfulness in light of Christ's return.

Believers in Rome had differing opinions about various foods and the importance of observing various holy days (14:1–15:13). They must show respect one for another (14:10) and be careful not to hinder the growth of other believers by offending their religious scruples. Their key concern must be to build up one another (vv. 19-21). They could follow the example of Christ, who gave up His own rights to serve others (15:1-13).

Final Comments (15:14–16:27)

Paul shared his personal plans to solicit their prayers and help. He would pass through Rome as he continued westward to Spain

(15:22-33). He commended Phoebe for her service to the church at Cenchrea and may have sent this letter by her (16:1-2). He issued a final warning about false teachers, added greetings from fellow believers with him in Corinth, and concluded with a doxology praising the wisdom of God in providing salvation to all nations (vv. 17-27).

A Key Text to Consider (12:1-8)

The teaching material is both related to and dependent on the theological foundation laid in the first section of the book. The phrase, "Therefore I urge you, brethren, by the mercies of God" in verse 1 links the two sections together.

The Twin Foundations for Gifted Service (vv. 1-2)

The presentation of the body and the transformation of the mind are twin foundations upon which the exercise of gifted service must be constructed. Before we look at these two ideas, we must look at the final phrase of verse 1 to understand the thrust of the section. Paul wanted the Romans to understand that one's "spiritual service of worship" is the presentation of the body to God. The Greek word is *logikos* and can be translated as "spiritual" or "reasonable." I prefer "reasonable," which indicates that the presentation of ourselves to God is the only "logical," or "normative" response when we consider the cost of our redemption.

The presentation of the body as our appropriate response of worship recalls the truth that God has made our bodies alive from the dead through the gift of His Son (Rom. 6:4-6). That which God has made alive from the dead is all He desires and all that He will receive. We sometimes think of worship as the gathering of believers on Sunday morning, but God views worship as an ongoing, everyday activity that requires the presentation of our bodies and thus our gifted service.

The mention of "living" sacrifice would have brought to mind the sacrificial system of the Old Testament. In contrast to "dead" animal sacrifices, Christians are expected to present our bodies as living sacrifices. All we have to offer Him is the body He has made alive, a truth established in Romans 6:13. Those who have received mercy are now empowered to express mercy through bodies that have been made alive by the resurrection and gifted by God's Spirit!

The three qualifying words: "living," "holy," and "acceptable," are of equal value and define the presentation of our bodies. "Living" sacrifice is made possible precisely because our bodies have been raised from the dead and granted newness of life (6:4). "Living" also indicates that giving our bodies is a daily and ongoing gift.

"Holy" underlines both the totality of the sacrifice and its ethical character. As Christians, our bodies are separated unto the Lord, and we no longer make claims as to how or when we serve. Everything we are and everything we have is at His disposal. Our service to the King should reveal His holiness, pointing to Him and not to the gifted servant.

The presentation of our bodies is "acceptable" in the sense that it is what God requires and only what He will accept. Anything less is insufficient and inappropriate. This word also carries the Lord's affirmation. God has already declared your service is "acceptable" or "pleasing." *God has made you for Himself, redeemed you by His grace, and gifted you by His Spirit to join Him in the earthly advance of His kingdom.*

The second pillar is transformation through the renewing of the mind. Since we live and serve in the world, we must guard against being conformed to the values of the present age. The world tells us life is about us. It convinces us that we are number one and that the present life is all that matters. If we buy into this value system, we will allow the world to squeeze us into its mold. The Bible teaches that the present order is passing away but that we are citizens of "a kingdom which cannot be shaken" (Heb. 12:28).

The antidote to conformity is transformation by the renewal of the mind. As we comprehend who we are in Christ and our Kingdom potential based on our gifts, our passion to serve the King is intensified. Christians who are made alive by the Spirit but never submit themselves to God in service are often sucked back into the tyrannizing power of the world.

Our thinking impacts our behavior. The renewal of the mind allows us to see ourselves from God's vantage point. It enables us to recognize the gracious character of all life and thus to anticipate the work of the Holy Spirit in our lives. The Holy Spirit provides the supernatural resources we need to serve the King effectively, thus proving the will of God. "Prove" means that we can discern the will of God and accomplish it.

The Principle of Sound Judgment (v. 3)

Paul first cautions that when we evaluate our gifted potential we must guard against overevaluation. Spiritual gifts can create spiritual pride. When someone sees his or her gift as a sign of advanced spirituality, it leads to destructive behavior, which negatively impacts unity.

Paul not only cautions about overevaluation; he insists that everyone should practice sound judgment based on the truth that "God has allotted to each a measure of faith." Those who argue they have no gifts to offer become *consumers* of grace without ever becoming *contributors* to the Kingdom. It is significant that Paul addressed them "through the grace given to me." This phrase was not intended to give apostolic authority to Paul's appeal but rather to underline his dependence upon God's grace for life and ministry.

Notice the emphatic use of "each," indicating that "a measure of faith" has been "allotted" to each member of the body of Christ. The emphasis is on the individuality and uniqueness of each portion and not on the quantity of the gift. The same idea is taught in 1 Corinthians 12:18, where Paul asserted that each member of the body has been placed there by unique design. "Measure of faith" means the comprehension of one's gifted potential and the accompanying understanding of the role of gifts in the advance of the Kingdom. Each of us must discover our unique and assigned task to perform.

The Principle of Unity through Diversity (vv. 4-5)

Verses 4 and 5 indicate that diversity is the key to unity. Paul employed the picture of the human body to illustrate the proper working of the gifted community. The human body functions as a unified whole because it is made up of a variety of members, each with a unique and yet indispensable function. When any member fails to serve in his or her given role, the entire body is impeded in its mission. Conversely, no one member can fulfill all the functions in the body.

Maybe you think your gift and role in the body of Christ are insignificant and that no harm will be done if you fail to serve. Nothing could be further from the truth. All members are equally important. Our King makes no mistakes; you were created, redeemed, and gifted so that your life and service would have eternal impact.

The Principle of Interdependence (v. 5b)

The phrase "individually members one of another" breaks the parallelism with verse 4 and thus stands out in bold relief. Gifts should never lead to spiritual pride and isolation, for they actually mean that we are interdependent. Our fallen human nature drives us to independence.

God created us to be relational beings, and therefore we will always need to be a part of community. Discovering our own unique, gifted identity should not lead us to arrogant isolation but rather to responsible Christian community. When we understand who we are in Christ, we no longer have to be all things to all people. The compulsion to prove ourselves to others is no longer the quest of our life. The loneliness of isolation is replaced by the companionship of authentic community.

We cannot function independently, because God created us, uniquely gifted us, and placed us in the body just as He chose. You are part of a larger community by creation and by redemption.

The Principle of Universal Giftedness (vv. 6-8)

This entire section is based on the understanding that every believer is gifted. The phrase "Since we have gifts that differ according to the grace given to us" is clear indication that no one is excluded. The variety of gifts is important to the unity of the body. Each member has a role to play, and each is important to the proper functioning of the body.

Paul then included a gift list that is intentionally broad. It includes a few gifts we might expect to find, such as prophecy and teaching. Service, leading, and exhorting are different than those included in 1 Corinthians 12, but somewhat expected. Giving and showing mercy are a bit more unexpected in a gift list. This list shows the breadth of functions that Paul considered to be spiritual gifts. None of the various lists of gifts found in the Pauline letters is intended to be comprehensive, only illustrative.[1]

The Principle of the Common Good

In the Greek verse 6 requires that we add a verbal statement such as "each of us is to exercise them accordingly." Gifts are not given by God for our amusement or the amazement of our friends. They have meaning and purpose only when they are employed through His church for His kingdom and glory. This assures us that God has sovereignly equipped His church to accomplish His work in every generation. No task is too great for the church that will assist its members in discovering and using their gifts.

There are many wonderful truths we can take away from this passage. You a part of God's gifted body. You were created and gifted to be a co-laborer with Christ. No person is unimportant or insignificant in the work of the church. Your life matters to God.

For Memory and Meditation

"Therefore I urge you, brethren, by the mercies of God, to present your bodies a living and holy sacrifice, acceptable to God, which is your spiritual service of worship." (Rom. 12:1)

---

[1] If you are interested in knowing more about gifts, consider the twelve-week DVD study *You Are Gifted*, available through Auxanopress.com.

Chapter 7

Colossians

Focal Passage: Colossians 1:13-23

Paul refers to his imprisonment in four of his letters—Colossians, Ephesians, Philemon, and Philippians. These letters are frequently referred to as the Prison Epistles. Some commentators suggest that the word *captivity* might be more appropriate, since Paul was actually awaiting trial and was allowed to have visitors. The most likely place of imprisonment was Rome.

Three of the letters—Colossians, Ephesians, and Philemon— are closely linked together and were written in the same place and nearly at the same time. Tychicus and Onesimus were the couriers who transported all three of these letters from Rome (Eph. 6:21; Col. 4:7-9). The similarities in content in the Ephesian and Colossian letters indicate they were written one after the other. The Philemon letter was prompted by the presence of Onesimus, a runaway slave, who had become a believer and close friend of Paul's while in prison (Philem. 10-16).

Where Was Paul? Why Did He Write Colossians?

Paul was on his way to Jerusalem with the offering for the saints. After a moving farewell to the leaders of the church at Ephesus, he sailed to Jerusalem. Luke alerts us to the fact that Paul was aware that his trip to Jerusalem would lead to difficult circumstances, possibly even his own death (Acts 20:25).

The leaders in Jerusalem gladly received Paul as they heard his report about the response among the Gentiles. They warned him that he might be facing trouble from some men who were zealous for the Jewish law and had given out a false report that Paul was teaching Jewish converts to forsake the law and customs of Moses (21:21). The leaders suggested that Paul take a temporary Nazarite vow to prove himself a keeper of the law (vv. 23-24, 26).

When the seven days of the vow were complete, Paul accompanied the men into the temple. Some Jews from Asia saw Paul there and began to stir up the crowd, claiming that Paul had brought Greeks into the temple. They had previously seen Trophimus, a Gentile from Ephesus, in the city with Paul and jumped to the conclusion that Paul had taken him into the temple (vv. 27-29).

The crowd drug Paul out of the temple, seeking to kill him. To stop the angry crowd, a Roman commander bound Paul with chains and took him to the fortress. When Paul revealed that he was a Roman citizen, he was allowed to speak, and he gave his testimony about his conversion and mission (ch. 22).

Paul was brought before the Sanhedrin. The Council was divided, and a great dissension developed, prompting the commander to take Paul to the barracks for his own safety. The Lord confirmed to Paul that he would bear witness to Him at Rome (23:10-11). More than forty of the zealous Jews took a vow to kill Paul. Paul's nephew informed him of the plot, which led the commander to move Paul to Caesarea (vv. 12-16, 23-24).

Paul was delivered to Felix along with a letter of explanation from Claudius Lysias (vv. 26-31). The high priest Ananias came from Jerusalem along with some elders to bring charges against Paul. Felix had knowledge about the Christian movement and summed up the situation accurately. Since there were conflicting statements, he kept Paul in custody with a reasonable amount of freedom (24:1, 22-23).

Paul remained on house arrest for two years. When Porcius Festus succeeded Felix, the Jews again made their case against Paul, and Festus agreed to hear them in Caesarea. The Jews brought unsubstantiated charges against Paul; but to curry the favor of the Jews, Festus asked Paul if he would go to Jerusalem to stand trial. Knowing it was a trap, Paul invoked his right as a Roman citizen and appealed to Caesar (24:27–25:12).

After an eventful journey marked by storms, a shipwreck, and a miraculous visit on Malta, Paul arrived safely in Rome. Paul was allowed to stay by himself with a soldier who was guarding him (28:16). Luke ended his narrative with the two-year house imprisonment.

Epaphras, a Pauline convert and founder of the Colossian church, was one of Paul's visitors in Rome (Col. 1:7-8; 4:12-13). The Colossian church was likely founded during the time of Paul's Ephesian ministry (around AD 53–55). A dangerous heresy was impacting the church at Colossae. The false teaching was syncretistic in nature, and thus Paul did not present a systematic response but dealt with the different elements, which, at times, appear to be contradictory.

As with most heretical systems, the false teachers did not accept the full deity and supremacy of Christ. Paul warned his readers not to be led astray by human philosophy and empty speculation. Further, there were some persons who wanted to impose legalistic Jewish practices such as circumcision, dietary regulations, religious festivals, and human traditions (2:8, 11, 16). Asceticism, which imposed restrictions on the body and demanded abstinence, was also promoted by the false teachers (vv. 21-23).

Finally, the worship of angels as intermediaries between God and the physical universe was present (v. 18).

Compelled by the Spirit, Paul seized upon the visit of Epaphras and the church's need to pen the Colossian letter to correct false teaching and exalt Christ's person and work. Colossians is therefore one of the most Christocentric letters of the New Testament.

Placing the letter during the Roman imprisonment would mean a date around AD 62 or 63. Paul wrote to a church he had not planted to express his personal interest in them and to refute the false teaching threatening the churches in the Lycus Valley.

An Overview of the Letter

Like so many of the Pauline letters, Colossians has a section on theology or doctrine followed by one of application or ethical application. Correct theology should be evidenced in ethical behavior, which emerges naturally from it.

Salutation, Thanksgiving, and Prayer (1:1-12)

Paul began with a salutation similar to those of his other letters. It identifies Paul the apostle along with Timothy as the author and sender of the letter. It is addressed "to the saints and faithful brethren" in Colossae. The greeting "Grace to you and peace" is a Christianized variant of the regular Greek salutation.

Paul's traditional word of thanksgiving referenced the faith and love of the Colossians. He mentioned his unceasing prayers for the church, with special attention to his desire that they "be filled with the knowledge of His will in all spiritual wisdom and understanding" (v. 9). This would allow them to live in a worthy manner, bearing fruit and increasing in knowledge, strengthened with power for attaining all steadfastness.

The Person and Work of Christ (1:13–2:7)

This section is at the heart of the letter as Paul proclaimed the supremacy of Christ to counter the false teachers. He emphasized that Christ is Redeemer, supreme over creation, Sustainer of the universe, and head of the church (1:17-18). Since the fullness of God resides in Christ, He alone can reconcile humanity to the Father (vv. 19-20).

Having spoken of Christ in relation to the church, Paul then mentioned his ministry, since the Colossians would not have known Paul personally. He insisted that his sufferings and ministry through the church were a part of his stewardship toward them as a Gentile congregation (vv. 24-29). His concern was that they would develop unity of love and a complete understanding of Christ. He affirmed that all the treasures of wisdom and knowledge were found in Christ so that no one would delude them with persuasive arguments (2:1-7).

The Antidote to False Teaching (2:8–3:4)

Since all the fullness of God dwells in Him, believers do not need to worship any supernatural being (2:8-15). In verses 16-23 Paul warned against submission to legalism. If the Colossians submitted to Jewish regulations, they were allowing the opinions of humans to dominate their behavior. Since they had been released from the power of any other supernatural being, other than Jesus, it would be foolish to put themselves under the rules and authority of a defeated enemy.

Those who have been raised up with Christ are to seek the things above where Christ is seated at the right hand of God. Believers are to keep their minds focused on heavenly realities rather than earthly ones (3:1-2).

The Christian Life (3:5–4:6)

The new life Paul had just described must be evidenced in Christian behavior. Paul demanded that they "put to death" immorality, impurity, lust, evil desire, and greed (3:5 CSB). These were behaviors characteristic of their pre-Christian existence and were inconsistent with new life in Christ. Another list of behaviors that would threaten community, including anger, wrath, malice, slander, and filthy language, are presented as equally dangerous (vv. 5-11 CSB).

Believers must not only put to death old habits; they must put on positive traits such as compassion, kindness, humility, gentleness, and patience. The zenith is love, which results in peace throughout the Christian community (vv. 12-17).

The new life will manifest itself at home. Paul called upon husbands to love wives, wives to respect their husbands, and children to obey their parents. Parents must avoid harsh discipline, which could embitter their children. Slaves should offer sincere obedience, and masters must treat slaves with justice. Every relationship should be governed by one's desire to please the Lord (3:18–4:1).

Paul concluded with a call to devoted and alert prayer, maintained in an attitude of thanksgiving. He requested prayer for himself, specifically asking for an open door and clarity in preaching the gospel (4:2-4).

Personal Notes and Final Greetings (4:7-18)

Paul spoke of the upcoming visit by Tychicus and Onesimus to Colossae. They would give more complete information about his circumstances (vv. 7-9). Paul included greetings from friends who supported him during his confinement. He encouraged them to share this letter with the Christians in Laodicea and to expect his letter, which would soon be coming from them (vv. 10-17).

A Key Text to Consider (1:13-23)

There were several elements to the heresy that was threatening the church at Colossae, but by far the most dangerous was the depreciation of the person of Jesus Christ. To the false teachers, Christ was not the triumphant Redeemer to whom all authority in heaven and earth had been given. To them, he was one of the many spirit beings who served as bridge between God and humans.

Knowing where the passage on the supremacy of Christ begins and the prayer (vv. 3-14) ends is actually difficult. For our study, we will begin with the final affirmation of Paul's opening prayer, since it establishes the basis for the profound declaration on the uniqueness of Jesus to provide redemption and forgiveness. Paul would next deal with the scope of Christ's supremacy (vv. 15-18) and its basis (vv. 19-23). It is possible that the section beginning with verse 15 is an early Christian teaching or hymn, similar to Philippians 2:5-11.

Rescued, Transferred, Redeemed, and Forgiven (vv. 13-14)

These four theologically charged words explain how the Father qualified sinful mankind to share in the "inheritance of the saints in Light" stated in verse 12. First, God delivered or "rescued" us from the domain of darkness (v. 13). The obvious contrast between "light" and "darkness" should not be overlooked. Darkness is symbolic of ignorance, falsehood, and sin. It is the miserable state that humans in sin experience now and for eternity. The word "domain" is the power or dominion that evil exercises over humans. Since all humans have sinned, all live under the dominion of sin.

Second, He "transferred us to the kingdom of His beloved Son." The idea is that of moving from one country and settling as a citizen in another. The verb tense points to a definitive time of one's conversion, which established new citizenship. That which will one day be our new habitation has already become reality for the believer.

Third, we have redemption and forgiveness by virtue of our union with Christ (v. 14). *Redemption* is a biblical term that speaks of a release purchased with the payment of a price. It was used to speak of the deliverance of slaves from bondage or prisoners from captivity. Our redemption is accompanied by the forgiveness of sins. The image is of the removal of our sins so that they no longer serve as a barrier that separates sinful humanity from holy God.

Christ's Supremacy over Creation (vv. 15-18)

Here, Paul presented Christ as God's unique agent, from his primeval work of creation through the redemption at midpoint to the new creation, which will occur at the consummation. The affirmation of Christ's supremacy clearly refuted the false teachers who looked to angelic mediators. In the light of growing heresy, it was critical for Paul to pay particular attention to the cosmic significance of Christ.

The phrase "the image of the invisible God" is a clear declaration of Christ's eternal deity. Since Christ is eternally God, He was in the image of God from eternity past; as Christ incarnate, He brought God's image into earthly view; and in heaven He will bear the image as the exalted Lord (cf. John 17:1-6).

Two ideas are expressed by the term *image*; the first is "likeness." Christ is the exact likeness of God, just as the image on a coin expresses exactly the imprint on the die (cf. Heb. 1:3). The second idea is that of "manifestation," a concept presented clearly in John 1:18: "No one has seen God at any time; the only begotten God who is in the bosom of the Father, He has explained Him." In the Incarnation, Christ made the invisible God visible; in Him the nature and being of God are perfectly and completely revealed. Quite a contrast to the vague and shadowy intermediaries revered by the false teachers.

In the second half of verse 15 Paul turned his focus to Christ's supremacy over creation. The context prohibits the suggestion that "firstborn" can imply that Christ was the first of the created order, suggesting He was created at some point in time. Far from being part of creation, He is the One through whom creation came to be (v. 16).

"Firstborn" affirms Christ's *supremacy* in terms of rank and His *priority* in terms of time. He was/is before creation, and He is Lord of all creation, since He is Creator and Sustainer (vv. 16-17). This same term will be used again in verse 18; in Revelation 1:5, where He is declared to be "the firstborn of the dead"; and in Romans 8:29 as the "firstborn among many brethren." The writer of Hebrews speaks of God bringing "the firstborn into the world" (1:6), affirming His eternal Sonship that was revealed through incarnation.

There may also be an allusion to the ancient custom whereby a family accorded rights and privileges to the firstborn that were not given to other children. The firstborn was the father's representative and primary heir who had the responsibility for the management of the household. Christ fulfills all of these roles in relationship to the Father.

Verses 16 and 17 affirm that Christ is Lord over creation because everything was created "by Him," "through Him," and "for Him." The preposition *by* indicates He is the agent of creation.

Some translations say "in Him," indicating He is the very sphere in which creation occurred. Both are possible and both are true. The preposition *through* emphasizes that Christ is the agent through which everything came into being. It is "for Him," meaning it is moving toward its ultimate consummation in Him. Everything exists to serve His purpose and contribute to His glory.

The clear implication is that the present universe, which includes things in the heavens and on earth, visible and invisible, thrones or dominions, and rulers and authorities, has no authority over the person who is in Christ. This is a clear response to the Colossian heresy and the angelic hierarchy that was so prominent in later gnostic thought. Paul's mention of these various powers does not suggest he actually believed in this exact hierarchy of spirit beings. He was simply affirming that whatever authorities and powers existed on earth or in the heavens, Christ is the one who made them and thus is their Lord.

Verse 17 says, "He is before all things" in time and rank. Christ is the unifying principle and personal sustainer of creation. Without Him, the cosmos would disintegrate.

Christ's Supremacy over His Church (v. 18)

It may surprise you to discover that Paul considered Christ's Lordship over the church to be the zenith of His creative work. We often think of God's glory as being revealed in the beauty of the creation, but Paul affirmed that His greatest work of creation is seen in His church.

As "head," Christ is the source of its very existence and also its leader who alone has authority to direct and govern it. Curtis Vaughan commented that the image of the church as "the body" suggests three things. First, it is a living organism composed of members jointed vitally to one another. Second, it is the means by which Christ carries out His purposes and performs His work on earth. Third, it shows that the union between Christ and His people is intimate and vital. "Together they constitute one living unity, each, in a sense, being incomplete without the other."[1]

Paul used "firstborn" in relation to Christ once more with the emphasis now being on His creation of a new community of those who have been made alive together with Him—His church. Christ is the "beginning" and the "firstborn" in terms of resurrection, as He was in creation. His resurrection marked His total victory over all powers and authorities that held men in bondage. His resurrection was the promise and assurance of a great harvest day of resurrected believers. Final resurrection is anticipated by those who have eternal life through Him and thus are joined to His earthly body, His church. Being the firstborn from the dead established Christ's place as the origin of the church's life.

It is through His church that He "will come to have first place in everything." The church's very purpose is to extend Christ's kingdom to the ends of the earth until the end of the age, with the purpose that Christ will be victoriously and permanently declared as who He has always been—Lord. This emphasis on the church being the means by which Christ's Lordship is established does not diminish the Lordship of Christ; but it magnifies greatly the role of the church in being the God-appointed means by which Christ expands His kingdom until His return.

The Basis for Christ's Supremacy (vv. 19-23)

Verse 19 begins with the word "for," indicating that Paul was now giving the basis for Christ's supremacy. Simply stated, it was God's purpose, His "good pleasure" for the "fullness" to dwell permanently in Christ.

"Fullness" translates an important Greek word *pleroma*. This term has unique significance in the Colossian and Ephesian letters. It is likely that the word was used by the false teachers to denote the totality of supernatural powers that were in control of the lives of humanity. All communication between God and humans had to pass through the spheres in which these powers exercised authority. In this one statement Paul dismantled this whole system. The totality of divine essence and power are resident in Christ. Christ is God in all His fullness. For that reason He is the only mediator between God and humanity.

Further, it was God's good pleasure "to reconcile all things to Himself" through Christ (v. 20). The basic meaning of "reconcile" is to change one's relationship from enmity to friendship. "All things" suggests the widest possible scale and therefore means the whole universe as indicated by the phrase "things on earth or things in heaven." This does not mean that everything or everyone will be brought into a saving relationship with Christ. Such universalism stands against the clear teaching of Scripture. The main idea is the cosmic significance of Christ's redemptive work (cf. Rom. 8:19-22). One day, the disorder caused in creation by sin will be done away with. Even hostile powers will unwilling acknowledge His Lordship (Phil. 2:11).

Christ has accomplished this reconciling work "through the blood of His cross." This is a clear reference to the sacrificial aspect of Christ's death. Paul affirmed that reconciliation has been accomplished by an event that occurred in human history. It was a voluntary giving up of a righteous life of Christ on the cross in a sacrificial and redemptive purpose.

In the next several verses Paul explained and applied this personally. In their former condition the Colossians were alienated, hostile in mind, and engaged in evil deeds (v. 21). The means of their reconciliation was the death of Christ, with the ultimate and assured goal that they would stand before Him holy, blameless, and beyond reproach (v. 22). The evidence of their new relationship was their abiding faith in the gospel that Paul proclaimed (v. 23).

For Memory and Meditation

"For it was the Father's good pleasure for all the fullness to dwell in Him." (Col. 1:19)

---

[1] Curtis Vaughan, *Colossians: A Study Guide* (Grand Rapids, MI: Zondervan, 1973), 41.

Chapter 8

Ephesians

Focal Passage: Ephesians 1:15-23

Luke, in the book of Acts, makes it clear that Paul had a unique relationship with the Ephesian church. On his way to Jerusalem to deliver the offering for the saints, Paul stopped for a final visit with the leaders of the church at Ephesus.

God had revealed to Paul that his trip to Rome would be such that he would probably never see these dear friends again. The final scene is described by Luke. "When he had said these things, he knelt down and prayed with them all. And they began to weep aloud and embraced Paul, and repeatedly kissed him, grieving especially over the word which he had spoken, that they would not see his face again" (Acts 20:36-38a).

Ephesians reflects this same tender relationship between Paul and the church family. In this letter Paul allowed us to place our ear to the door of his prayer closet. The language is effusive as Paul poured out his heart in prayer and petition. He blessed God "who has blessed us with every spiritual blessing in the heavenly places in Christ" (1:3). God's blessings are not privileges to be consumed but are gifts to be shared. They enable the church to express God's fullness in the world today.

Where Was Paul? Why Did He Write Ephesians?

In the last chapter, I presented evidence for considering Colossians, Ephesians, and Philemon as a trio of letters written at the same time from Rome in the early 60s. When Epaphras visited Paul in Rome, he shared disturbing news that heretical teachers, who devalued the person and work of Christ, were troubling his church.

Paul responded quickly to the needs of the church at Colossae by writing them a letter and requesting specifically that they share it with the church at Laodicea (Col. 4:16). The Holy Spirit impressed upon Paul the need to address the concerns raised by the heresy spreading to other churches in proconsular Asia.

The most dangerous aspect of the heresy was the attack on the uniqueness of Christ as the one Mediator between God and humanity. Paul addressed that issue directly in Colossians. In Ephesians he considered the potential impact an attack on the person of Christ could have on our understanding of the church.

The church's mission is to declare the gospel, which focuses on the uniqueness of Christ as the Redeemer of humanity. If Christ is simply one among many mediators between God and humans, the church is no more unique than any other of the multitude of mystery religions. By way of application, we could say that if the church's message is not unique, then the church is little more than a divine country club.

I believe that Ephesians was intended to be shared with all the churches in proconsular Asia. If one church was threatened by the heretical teachings, all were at risk. There are several clues in Colossians and Ephesians that suggest both letters were intended as circular letters.

Tychicus was Paul's companion who transported the trio of letters (Eph. 6:21-22; Col. 4:7). The trip from Rome to Ephesus would have been made by ship. When Tychicus arrived at Ephesus, he would have been carrying the three letters and would have been accompanied by Onesimus. Because the slave was fair game for bounty hunters, Tychicus would have left the letter in Ephesus with instructions to share it with other churches in proconsular Asia and proceeded down the Lycus Valley directly to Colossae with Onesimus, carrying the letters to the Colossians and Philemon.

It has been suggested that the seven churches listed together in the book of Revelation were an early association of churches that joined together for mutual support. If we accept this suggestion, then we can surmise that the letter from Ephesus would have gone consecutively to Smyrna, Sardis, Thyatira, Pergamum, Philadelphia, and Laodicea. Each church would make a copy and then send the letter to the next church.

Likely, Ephesians is the letter the church at Colossae was expecting from the church at Laodicea (Col. 4:16). We can further suggest that the Colossian letter would not simply have been shared with the church at Laodicea but would have been shared with the seven churches that also received Ephesians. The two letters explain and complement one another.

If you have a study Bible with critical notes, you will find a note on Ephesians 1:1 that some early manuscripts do not contain the words "at Ephesus." This suggests that the original may have had a blank where each church could place their name to personalize the letter.

This proposed reconstruction also helps to explain a reference in Ephesians 3. Notice that Paul introduced himself as if the readers of Ephesians had never heard of him (vv. 1-2). When we remember the Acts account of his ministry in Ephesus, this reference seems strange. Paul also referred to a "mystery" that had been made known to him that he had written about "before in brief" (v. 3). When the Ephesian believers had the opportunity to read this further explanation of the "mystery," they would more fully understand what Paul meant by it.

To solve this riddle, we must ask what was written previously about the "mystery," which the Ephesian believers would have access to in the future. The most likely answer is Colossians 1:24-29. The mystery is the church made up of Jews and Gentiles, who can now comprehend together that Christ in them is the hope of glory.

Based on this reconstruction, we conclude that the Ephesian letter was written to the churches of proconsular Asia to complement and apply the truths taught in Colossians with a special emphasis on the church. Since Christ is unique, His church is God's household built upon the foundation of the apostles and prophets with Christ as the cornerstone (2:20-23). The church is the instrument through which God will exhibit His manifold wisdom to the rulers and authorities in the heavenly places (3:9-11). Thus, Ephesians was written shortly after Colossians from Paul's house imprisonment.

An Overview of the Letter

The content of Ephesians falls into two divisions. Chapters 1–3 discuss the spiritual privileges of believers and their application to the church, and chapters 4–6 discuss the responsibility of members of the body for a Christian walk in church, community, and family.

Salutation and the Spiritual Blessings Available in Christ and through His Church (1:1–3:21)

Paul began with his usual introduction (1:1-2) and then discussed all the blessings available to believers in Christ (vv. 3-14). The key to understanding this section is to notice the various phrases that indicate that the blessings are "in Christ," "in Him," "through His blood," and "in the Beloved" (vv. 5-7). God has predestined that those in Christ will inherit these blessings, which include holiness, adoption as sons, redemption, forgiveness, and an inheritance. The listing of blessings is intended to cause the reader to ask how one can find his or her place "in Him" where all the blessings reside. The answer is found in verse 13, which involves hearing and responding to the gospel.

Paul prayed that his readers would understand the hope of God's calling, the riches of the glory of His inheritance in the saints, and the surpassing greatness of His power toward believers (vv. 15-19). He elaborated on the power that raised Jesus from the dead and placed every authority, power, and dominion under His feet for the church, "which is His body, the fullness of Him who fills all in all" (vv. 20-23). This word "fullness" is the same word used to describe Christ in Colossians 1:19.

In Ephesians 2:1-10 Paul described the condition of sinful mankind without Christ. Humanity's sinful condition was met with God's mercy based on His unlimited love. While we were dead in our sins, He made us alive through His grace "and seated us with Him in the heavenly places in Christ Jesus" (v. 6). Salvation is by grace alone, through faith alone. The implications of salvation for spiritual community are profound (vv. 11-22). Jews and Gentiles are made into one new person because both have been reconciled to God and one another through the cross. This new community is God's household, his holy temple, which is "being built together into a dwelling of God in the Spirit" (v. 22).

In 3:1-14 Paul spoke of his unique ministry in unveiling a mystery that had been hidden for ages. That mystery involves the creation of the church, made up of Jew and Gentile. This community will make known the wisdom of God to the rulers and authorities in the heavenly places. The church was the eternal plan of God, carried out in Christ Jesus our Lord. This leads to a second prayer (vv. 14-21) in which Paul prayed for the church to be strengthened, know the love of Christ, and be filled up to the "fullness" of God (v. 19).

The Responsibilities and Privileges of the Christian (4:1–6:24)

Paul began by explaining how the gifted community functions, enabling it to demonstrate the "fullness" of God. He first declared the sevenfold unity of the church (4:1-6), followed by the distribution of grace gifts for ministry. The focus is on gifted leaders who, in turn, equip gifted members for ministry. Such ministry leads to unity, maturity, and the growth of the body. The second half of chapter 4 (vv. 17-32) focuses on the behavior of believers in relationship with other believers. Believers must be renewed in mind and put on the new self, characterized by righteousness and holiness of truth.

In 5:1-21 Paul discussed the new walk of believers, paying particular attention to its impact on the church's mission. They are to be imitators of God and walk in love, which requires the giving up of oneself. By necessity, such a walk will rule out immorality, impurity, greed, filthiness, silly talk, and coarse jesting. The Christian walk will demonstrate the fruit of Light, which consists of goodness, righteousness, and truth, which pleases the Lord.

Paul then presented a new vision for the home (5:22–6:9). The relationship of husband and wife mirrors that of Christ and His church. This primary relationship in the home requires honor and love. Children are to obey parents, while parents are to discipline and instruct children with God's ultimate purpose in mind. Workers and employers are to relate in a manner that pleases the Lord.

Since these new relationships in Christ are radical and demand supernatural empowering, Paul outlined the strength available to believers as we don the armor of God (6:10-20). His conclusion contains a plea that the Ephesians pray for all the saints, including Paul in his mission work. Verses 21-24 give final details about the role of Tychicus and a brief benediction.

A Key Text to Consider (1:15-23)

In many of Paul's letters, he indicated that he had prayed constantly for the church since the day he founded it. Wouldn't you like to know how he interceded on behalf of his churches? Ephesians gives us a unique opportunity to listen to Paul pray.

Paul's Prayer Strategy (vv. 15-18a)

How easy it is to overlook little connecting phrases in Scripture, but each word is important and intentional. This section begins with "for this reason," a phrase linking Paul's passionate prayer with the section that precedes it. Because Christians have received abundant blessings, providing incredible Kingdom potential, Paul prayed that his readers would fully comprehend and embrace all available resources.

Paul indicated that his prayers had been prompted by reports of their "faith in the Lord Jesus" (v. 15). The fact that he has only "heard" of the faith of some of the recipients of this letter is further indication that it was intended for distribution beyond Ephesus.

The phrase "faith in the Lord Jesus which exists among you" is a direct reference to the conversion of the recipients through the preaching of the gospel. Their "love for all the saints" was indisputable evidence of the authenticity of their faith. True conversion not only establishes a personal relationship to God; it also alters one's relationship to others, particularly members of the household of faith.

The underlying passion of Paul's prayer is defined by the request that God would give believers "a spirit of wisdom and of revelation in the knowledge of Him" (v. 17). "Spirit" refers to the human spirit informed by the Holy Spirit. The word "wisdom" is listed first because the truths of the gospel, accessible only through revelation, are so overwhelming and wonderful it is impossible for humans to comprehend them unless they are willing to be taught by God.

Paul is not praying that believers would acquire more knowledge of certain truths about God but that they would grow "in the knowledge of Him." We can know about God and yet not know God. Personal knowledge of God leads to life in fellowship with Him.

The One who hears and responds to our prayers is described here as "the God of our Lord Jesus Christ, the Father of glory." The phrase indicates that the one true God is the God whom Jesus both acknowledges as God and reveals to us. Jesus readily spoke of the Father as "My God" (Matt. 27:46; John 20:17). This phrase does not suggest that Jesus is less than God.

The prayer begins with the plea that "the eyes of your heart may be enlightened" (v. 18a). Man without God is darkened in his understanding and thus behaves based on the futility of his mind (cf. Eph. 4:17-18). Believers are renewed in the spirit of their mind (cf. 4:23) and can understand God's word and will. The "heart" stands for the inner man in his entirety, the seat of intelligence and will. Paul is not praying for head knowledge that *informs* but heart knowledge that *transforms.* He then made three requests that are staggering in breadth.

The Hope of His Calling (v. 18b)

The calling of God speaks of His choice of His people "in Christ" before the foundation of the world. God has predetermined that all of salvation with its blessings would reside in Christ (v. 5). For that reason, Paul could speak of God choosing us "in Him before the foundation of the world" (v. 4). God's calling is made effective as persons respond to His call to everyone through "the message of truth, the gospel of your salvation" (v. 13).

God's calling speaks first of His initiative in salvation as He convicts us of sin and brings persons to Christ. In terms of redemption, His calling to salvation was an accomplished fact for the recipients of this letter. God's calling also has a present-tense context as He calls believers to a lifelong vocation of service. Since our calling comes from Eternal God, it brings to us an expectation and hope of an eternal destiny, and thus Paul spoke of "the hope of His calling" (v. 18b).

The Riches of the Glory of His Inheritance in the Saints (v. 18c)

In the Old Testament, God spoke often of Israel as His unique possession through whom He desired to manifest His name so that the nations would be drawn to Him (cf. Ex. 19:5-6). This privilege and responsibility is now applied to believers, who Paul has already addressed as "saints" (v. 1) and "God's own possession" (v. 14). We are God's heritage—His own possession through whom He will bring glory to Himself by accomplishing His kingdom agenda on earth.

What does it mean to you to contemplate the truth in verse 18c that God considers you "the glory of His inheritance"?

God has determined to advance His kingdom on earth and thus manifest His glory through His church. We must continually ask ourselves, "Are we reflecting His glory by advancing His kingdom?"

The Surpassing Greatness of His Power toward Us Who Believe (vv. 19-23)

Our calling and commission are of such consequence that Paul prayed for our understanding of the vast power "toward us who believe" (v. 19). This odd-sounding phrase means the power available to us and thus working through us. The phrase "the working of the strength of His might" makes clear that we are contemplating supernatural empowering.

Paul found words such as *dunamis* (power), *energia* (working), *kratos* (strength), and *ischys* (might) to be inadequate for explaining the power available through Christ's resurrection. He modified the description of power by using a participle translated as "surpassing greatness." This word is unique to Paul. It occurs twice in 2 Corinthians, one to describe the surpassing glory of the new covenant (3:10) and later to speak of the generosity of giving as evidence of "the surpassing grace of God in you" (9:14). The only other references are in Ephesians 2:7 and 3:19. Simply stated, the power available to His church surpasses description!

Paul moved to the one supreme event that demonstrated the power "toward us": the power that raised Jesus from the dead and seated Him at the right hand of the Father. The raising of the Son demonstrated the Father's approval, affirms Jesus as the Son, and declares Him Lord of all (Acts 4:10; 17:31; Rom. 1:4). The cross is the supreme demonstration of God's love, and the cross is the supreme demonstration of His power.

The Father "seated [His Son] at His right hand in the heavenly places" (Eph. 1:20), which is the repository of all spiritual blessings. Christ's ascension is a clear declaration of His power to forgive sin (Heb. 1:3; 1 Pet. 3:21-22) and to keep His followers secure for all eternity (Col. 3:1-4). The reference to God's right hand is to be understood in terms of power and authority by which the exalted King administers the government of heaven and earth. Paul alluded to Psalm 110:1, which has its supreme and ultimate fulfillment in the ascension of Christ.

Paul elaborated on all other powers and authorities by stating both positively and negatively. In verse 21 the emphasis is on the exaltation, whereas in verse 22 he drew attention to the subjection of all things to Christ. It is possible that the phrase "rule and authority and power and dominion" may have some application to the powers venerated by the false teachers. Paul was unconcerned with their labels or supposed powers. Whatever powers exist in the seen or unseen world, in this age or the one to come, one thing is certain—Christ is the sovereign Lord.

The only difference between this age and the age to come is that in the coming age His authority will be on open display. The world rulers of darkness, mentioned again in 6:12, exercise some power in the present age through deceit and darkness, but in the coming age they will have no power.

Verse 22 restates and summarizes all that has been said, using a reference to Psalm 8:6 that speaks of God's original plan for mankind's dominion over creation: "You make him to rule over the works of Your hands; / You have put all things under his feet." Through sin, humans lost this position of dominion over creation. Only one true Man, Christ Jesus, fulfilled God's divine purpose. Now through Him and in Him we are restored to our true dignity and purpose.

Paul concluded by declaring that all of this has been accomplished for the church, "which is His body, the fullness of Him who fills all in all" (v. 23). Christ is the supreme head of the church.

"Head" speaks of authority and also to the vital union between Christ and His church. This union is further emphasized by the phrase "which is His body."

The church as "body" is unique to Paul. It signifies the living power that unites the people of God to Christ and to one another. The life and power of the risen and exalted Christ flows through His church, and thus each member must function in obedience to Him.

Perhaps you remember the significance of the word "fullness" (*pleroma)* that we encountered in our study of Colossians 1:19. It is stunning to read that Paul would use the same word to describe the church that he used to describe Christ. The church is designed, called, and empowered to express the fullness of Christ as Christ expresses the fullness of God. The idea that the church can fully express Christ is not simply a beautiful ideal; it is the potential and purpose of the church.

With such power and so much at stake, why do we attempt and accomplish so little?

For Memory and Meditation

"And He put all things in subjection under His feet, and gave Him as head over all things to the church, which is His body, the fullness of Him who fills all in all." (Eph. 1:22-23)

Chapter 9

Philemon

Focal Passage: Philemon 10-22

Philemon is unique among the Pauline letters, as it is the most nearly private letter among the entire known Pauline collection. Its content was addressed most directly to Philemon, although Paul did include Apphia, Archippus, and the church that met in Philemon's house among those who were to read the letter (v. 2). This letter is a personal appeal on behalf of Onesimus, Philemon's slave who had become very dear to the apostle Paul.

The letter to Philemon is the shortest letter from Paul's hand, being composed of only twenty-five verses. Only Second John and Third John among the General Epistles are shorter, and Jude is essentially the same length. The length of Paul's letter to Philemon is explained by its singular desire—to secure freedom for Onesimus. In spite of its brevity and singularity of purpose, it is a letter of great value. It provides us with an intimate look at the aging apostle as he applied the gospel he had preached throughout his life. His message demonstrates genuine compassion for Onesimus and Philemon (vv. 7, 16) and his own integrity (v. 19). It provides a foundation upon which the church could build a foundation for the abolition of slavery.

Where Was Paul? Why Did He Write Philemon?

In our introduction to the Ephesian and Colossian letters, we have already hinted at the answer to the question posed by this brief letter that is primarily addressed to Philemon. We can build our reconstruction of the events from the evidence in the letter itself and its apparent connection to these other two letters. The mentions of Archippus in verse 2 and in Colossians 4:17 suggest that the recipients lived in Colossae. We cannot positively identify Archippus or Apphia, who are both mentioned in verse 2, but some speculate that Apphia may have been Philemon's wife, and Archippus their son.

We can surmise that Philemon was a leader of the church at Colossae. Paul's statement that Philemon owed him his own self (v. 19) implies that Paul viewed him as a spiritual son, either directly or indirectly. Possibly Philemon had heard Paul preach while in Ephesus. It is important to note that Paul referred to him as a "fellow worker" (v. 1).

In any case, God had somehow used the apostle or his preaching to bring conversion to Philemon's household. Philemon made his home available to other Christians for worship (v. 2), and his ministry had continually refreshed the hearts of the saints (v. 7). The possession of a home large enough to accommodate a house church and the ownership of slaves suggest Philemon was reasonably wealthy.

The most likely reconstruction would indicate that Onesimus had run away, apparently with money stolen from Philemon (v. 18). Some commentators suggest that Philemon had sent Onesimus on a mission from which he had failed to return. In either case, as a runaway slave, he had come into contact with the apostle Paul in Rome. It is entirely possible that he may have met Paul previously in the company of Philemon in Ephesus. If so, we can conjecture that Onesimus may have sought out a man whom he believed would help him in his time of need.

Paul seized the divine opportunity and led the runaway slave to the Lord. He referred to Onesimus as his child, "begotten in my imprisonment" and as his "very heart" (vv. 10, 12). As a believer, the slave who had been formerly "useless" to Philemon was now "useful" to Paul and Philemon. This is a bit of a play on words since *Onesimus* means "useful" or "profitable."

Paul's attachment to Onesimus, and his useful ministry to Paul, had resulted in Paul's desire to have Onesimus remain with him during his imprisonment. Paul, however, did not deem it appropriate to keep the slave in Rome without Philemon's permission (vv. 13-14). When Epaphras arrived in Rome with news of the heresy that was threatening the church in Colossae (Col. 4:12), Paul wrote Colossians and Ephesians to address the heretical teaching and to encourage the churches of proconsular Asia. Paul saw this as an opportunity to send Onesimus with Tychicus to deliver the two circular letters along with the letter to Philemon (cf. Col. 4:9).

The reference to Onesimus in Colossians 4:9 implies clearly that Paul viewed him as a fellow laborer and not as a slave. Rather than Tychicus returning the slave Onesimus to his owner, Paul indicated that Onesimus was serving Paul, the Colossian church, and the Lord, by joining Tychicus in informing them about the whole situation in Rome.

This reconstruction would suggest that Paul had several purposes in writing the letter to Philemon. First and foremost, he desired that Philemon forgive Onesimus and accept him as a brother in Christ rather than a household slave (vv. 16-17). Second, the tenor of the letter seems to indicate that Paul would prefer that Onesimus be sent back to Paul in Rome, unless he was soon released (vv. 20-21). Third, Paul desired to secure lodging with Philemon when released, as the result of their prayers

(v. 22). An overriding purpose of the letter was to strike at the very foundation of slavery by tactfully suggesting that Onesimus be considered a useful brother and not a slave.

Based on this reconstruction, Paul's letter to Philemon would have been written from prison in Rome in the early AD 60s.

An Overview of the Letter

The brevity of the letter to Philemon makes the outlining of the book a simple matter. Verses 1-3 provide a brief salutation. Verses 4-7 express gratitude for Philemon. Verses 8-21 are the heart of the letter and the appeal for the freedom of Onesimus. The concluding comments, greetings, and benediction are found in verses 22-25.

Paul began the letter with a personal greeting to Philemon, Apphia, Archippus, and the church meeting in Philemon's home. The greeting is a standard greeting with strong Christian overtones, as seen in many of Paul's letters.

He then expressed his thanksgiving for Philemon's faith and love for the Lord and for all the saints. His thanksgiving for Philemon and the church in his house led Paul to mention the content of his prayer that the fellowship of their faith might become effective through every good thing in them for Christ's sake.

Paul refused to utilize apostolic authority to order Philemon to do what was proper, but he appealed to him on the foundation of Christian love (vv. 8-9). He referred both to his age and his condition as a prisoner of Christ Jesus. Further, his appeal was based on his great love for the slave who had become his child through conversion.

Even though Paul knew that Philemon would want Onesimus to remain with Paul, he desired that Philemon act from his own free will and further suggested that God had used the temporary separation for good by giving Onesimus back as a brother forever (vv. 15-16).

Paul requested that Philemon treat Onesimus as he would the apostle himself, and he promised to stand good for any debt that Onesimus owed to Philemon. Without making a specific request for the slave's freedom, Paul expressed his confidence that Philemon would do more than Paul had asked (v. 21). He expressed his belief that he would soon be released, and he requested a guest room. He concluded with greetings from fellow believers and an expression of grace (vv. 23-25).

A Key Text to Consider (vv. 10-22)

The heart of the letter and Paul's appeal for Onesimus' freedom is found in verses 10 through 22. Since everything is vitally connected in this brief letter, it is important to note that the directions in this section are based on the relationship between Paul and Philemon. Paul's status as an apostle and his unique relationship to Philemon provided Paul with a strong platform for making a demand. Paul was aware that he could order Philemon to set Onesimus free, but he preferred to appeal to him based on love. Paul's appeal was not simply based on his age and status; it was based on Philemon's propensity to refresh the heart of fellow Christians (vv. 4-7).

Conversion—From Useless to Useful (vv. 10-11)

Paul crafted his appeal to touch Philemon's heartstrings. Before he referred to Onesimus by name, he mentioned his new status as a believer. Paul called him "my child . . . whom I have begotten in my imprisonment." The affection in the phrase "my child" should not be overlooked, nor should the pathos in the reference to Paul's present condition. Onesimus had a special place in the heart of the apostle because of his present condition.

We have already mentioned that Onesimus' name meant "useful." By the simple change from *euchrestos* to *achrestos* Paul played on the name of the slave to indicate that only at his conversion did Onesimus become what God had designed him to be. The contrast between Onesimus prior to conversion and after conversion is made even more clear in that he was formerly useless to one person but was now useful to two persons—"both to you and to me."

A slave that had shirked his duties, stolen from his master, and become a runaway had now become useful, working with a new attitude and purpose. Christian conversion should be marked by a radical transformation of behavior. Is there evidence that your life has changed from useless to useful?

An Appeal for the Return of Onesimus (vv. 12-16)

Paul now explained the pain caused by the decision to send Onesimus back to Philemon. The Greek word translated "send back" is the same word used in the narrative where Herod passed the responsibility back to Pilate for sentencing Jesus (Luke 23:7, 11). If we carry that same idea here, then Paul was not simply sending Onesimus back to his owner, but he was literally referring Onesimus' case to Philemon with the goal that his owner would set him free. The pathos of the phrase "my very heart" cannot be ignored. Onesimus had become very dear to the aging apostle, and thus it would be hard to imagine that Philemon could refuse Paul's request.

Paul stated his desire with clarity. He had wished to keep Onesimus with the goal that Onesimus could minister to Paul during his imprisonment. Paul was certain that were it possible, Philemon himself would have rendered service to Paul during his imprisonment. Since that was clearly not possible, Paul suggested that Onesimus would minister on Philemon's behalf.

Paul was convinced that Philemon would have gladly allowed Onesimus to stay (v. 14), but to have kept Onesimus without permission would have been manipulative in the utmost and thus a breach of Christian fellowship that demands mutual respect. "Compulsion" means an outward pressure exerted to make one act in a certain way, and thus it disrespects the rights and free will of a fellow believer. Can you think of instances when you have used manipulation to get your way in your church or small group?

It is difficult for us to know whether or not Paul actually intended that Philemon send Onesimus back to him. His request for a guest room seems to suggest that he expected to be released soon, which would enable him to enjoy the fellowship of both men in the near future (v. 22).

Paul then speculated as to God's redemptive purpose in the entire narrative of Onesimus' escape. Clearly the action of the slave in leaving Philemon and possibly stealing from him was wrong. Yet God, in His sovereignty, can redeem every circumstance. Paul was not justifying the sinful action of the slave. The use of "perhaps" in verse 15 is a statement of humility from the apostle who did not presume to know the mind of the Lord but was suggesting to Philemon that there may have been more going on in recent events than met the human eye.

Onesimus' trip to Rome and his encounter with Paul had led to his conversion. The verb translated "separated" is passive, possibly signifying the hidden action of God. God's greater purpose behind recent events would result in Philemon receiving Onesimus back forever. There is a difference of opinion as to how we should understand "forever." Some suggest it simply means "for good" or "permanently." But, given the context, "forever" seems more likely to suggest that now that Onesimus was a Christian brother, the new relationship between the two men would be eternal in nature.

Onesimus would return "no longer as a slave, but more than a slave, a beloved brother" (v. 16). He was especially so to Paul because the apostle had the privilege of leading Onesimus to the Lord. But in a sense he was more so to Philemon "both in the flesh and in the Lord." This curious phrase seems to mean in secular affairs and in spiritual matters. As a Christian, Onesimus would be more productive in his work (cf. Eph. 6:5-8) and also would be a productive Christian in terms of ministry.

We can see a parallel between this narrative and the wrongs suffered by Joseph at the hands of his brothers (Gen. 45:4-8). While the action of the brothers toward Joseph was clearly evil, God was at work sending Joseph to Egypt ahead of his family for their preservation. This corresponds with Paul's teaching in Romans 8:28 that God is bigger than man's evil intentions and actions. While God cannot and does not cause evil, He is capable of *causing all things to work together for good.* Paul wanted Philemon to see God's redemptive purpose in the recent events regarding Onesimus. Can you think of an example where God worked in a challenging event to bring a good result?

Refresh My Heart (vv. 17-21)

Paul then made his specific appeal. The word translated "partner" in verse 17 is the Greek word *koinonos,* suggesting Paul was not appealing to mere friendship. This word can be used of a business partnership as in Luke 5:10, but here it speaks of a deeper partnership based on a mutual relationship to Christ (1 Cor. 1:9). This relationship has drawn Paul and Philemon together in common activities for the gospel, and thus the idea is that of a coworker.

So Paul called upon Philemon to receive Onesimus as if he was receiving Paul himself. This corresponds with Paul's statement in verse 12 that sending Onesimus back was like sending his own heart. Further, based on our understanding of the significance of *koinonos*, Paul was appealing to Philemon to treat Onesimus as a fellow worker.

Paul was aware that Onesimus had likely taken money from his master to finance his trip to Rome. In addition, as a workman, he had robbed Philemon through lost labor. With that being the case, Paul instructed Philemon to "charge that to my account" (v. 18). Paul utilized commercial language to communicate his willingness to compensate Philemon for any loss he may have suffered.

The phrase "I, Paul, am writing this with my own hand" (v. 19) refers specifically to the note promising to repay Philemon for any loss. After personally signing his IOU, Paul reminded Philemon of the debt he owed to the apostle. It is likely that the phrase "even your own self" refers to Philemon's conversion. Perhaps Philemon had visited with Paul while he was preaching in Ephesus.

Paul strengthened his personal request by indicating that Philemon's treatment of Onesimus would benefit Paul by refreshing his heart. Paul was confident that Philemon would do even more than he asked (v. 21). We can't know for sure what "more" he expected. We would like to believe that Paul desired and expected Philemon to give Onesimus and his other slaves their freedom. The seeds of emancipation had certainly been sown in this brief letter, and we can thank God that the church, in time, took a strong stand against slavery. As Christians, we must continue to stand against all injustice.

For Memory and Meditation

"And I pray that the fellowship of your faith may become effective through the knowledge of every good thing which is in you for Christ's sake." (Philemon 6)

Chapter 10

Philippians

Focal Passage: 2:12-18

The Philippian letter is one of the more personal of Paul's letters, as he spoke candidly about his imprisonment and his struggle with life and death issues. He thanked the church for their support, spoke to the issue of dissension in the church, and called them to imitate Christ in all things.

Philippi was located in the northeast section of the Roman province. It was a city with a strategic location and abundant natural resources, including gold. Philip II of Macedon seized the valuable mining territory just after 400 BC and named the city for himself. Philip's son Alexander made Philippi the showpiece of Greek culture. Roman soldiers conquered Macedonia in 168 BC and divided the territory into four districts.

Paul visited Philippi on his second missionary journey, having been summoned to Macedonia as the result of a vision (Acts 16:6-12). According to Luke, Paul attended a Sabbath Day prayer meeting on the banks of the river, suggesting that the city had no synagogue. A businesswoman named Lydia was among the first converts in Macedonia. After she and her household were baptized, she implored Paul to remain as a guest in her home.

Paul's additional ministry in Philippi gives us further insight into the city's religious character. Paul freed a slave girl from demonic possession, and her owners dragged Paul and Silas into the marketplace, accusing them of teaching unlawful customs

(vv. 19-21). The missionaries were thrown into prison, where they proceeded to have a worship service. They were miraculously delivered by an earthquake but refused to leave the prison. The jailer was converted as a result of the events of that night (vv. 22-34).

On the day following the earthquake the chief magistrates sent policemen to release the prisoners (vv. 35-36). Paul refused to leave since he was a Roman citizen and therefore unlawfully retained. He insisted that the magistrates come in person and apologize (vv. 38-40). Paul's desire was to give credibility to the church and keep them from experiencing persecution after his departure.

Where was Paul? Why Did He Write Philippians?

Philippians is one of the Prison Epistles, and thus it was written from Rome during Paul's first Roman imprisonment. In Philippians 1 (vv. 7, 13) Paul spoke of his imprisonment, which had become known throughout the whole Praetorian Guard. This would refer to the emperor's bodyguard or praetorian cohorts stationed in the metropolis. Paul spoke of his deliverance but in such a manner that it was clear it could be through release or death (1:19-20; 2:17).

Likely, Paul wrote Philippians after Onesimus and Tychicus had departed for Ephesus on their mission. Perhaps Paul knew that his trial date was approaching; and although he anticipated a favorable verdict, he felt it expedient to send a letter to thank the church and to give details about his situation. This reconstruction would place the letter near the end of his two-year house imprisonment in the early AD 60s, soon after dispatching the other three Prison Epistles.

The letter provides sufficient clues that lead us to surmise that Paul had several interrelated reasons for posting this letter.

His greeting and opening paragraph often give us clear insight into his purpose for writing. In his prayer of thanksgiving, Paul mentioned his gratitude for their "participation in the gospel from the first day until now" (1:5).

The church had sent Epaphroditus to Rome with a financial gift for Paul. During his visit in Rome, Epaphroditus had become seriously ill (2:25-27; 4:18). Now that he had recovered, Epaphroditus was ready to return, and Paul wanted to ensure he was given appropriate honor. Paul's concluding section provides more specific and detailed mention of the consistent financial support this church had provided. The most recent gift, delivered by Epaphroditus, was simply a renewal of concern, which Paul's imprisonment had made possible. While Paul had found God's provision sufficient for all his needs, the generosity of this church had been consistent and noteworthy in light of the fact that after he left Macedonia this church alone had supported him (4:11-20).

Paul wanted to inform the Philippians of Timothy's impending visit and prepare them for the possibility that he desired to come in person when released from prison (2:19, 24). The tenor of the letter indicates that some in Philippi had concerns and anxieties about Paul's imprisonment. He wanted to ease their anxiety and remove any opportunity for adversaries to use his imprisonment against the church (1:12-18).

The necessity of a visit by Timothy may have been prompted by the news of some disunity among members and challenges from false teachers. Paul dealt with disunity by calling the Philippians to embody the attitude manifested by Christ in His incarnation (2:5-11, 19). He specifically calls on two women to live in harmony in the Lord (4:2).

The mention of "false circumcision" in 3:2 may suggest Judaizers had visited Philippi, but the brevity of the mention indicates their presence had not had the impact it did in Galatia. Another group of persons reflected a tendency toward sensuality and greed (vv. 17-21). He called upon them to set their minds on heavenly things.

An Overview of the Letter

This letter opens with the traditional salutation (1:1-2). Paul identified himself and Timothy as coauthors. He mentioned both the Philippian believers and their leaders. The two leadership groups reflect a consistent New Testament pattern of "overseers" (sometimes referred to as pastors or elders) and "deacons." His prayer of thanksgiving in verses 3-11 indicates his great affection for this congregation.

God's Providence and Paul's Imprisonment (1:12–2:18)

The next extended section deals with Paul's welfare during his imprisonment with special attention given to God's providence in working His "good" in spite of difficult circumstances. First, Paul's confinement had actually accelerated the spread of the gospel. Paul realized that some were teaching from wrong motives, but he rejoiced as long as Christ was preached (1:12-18). Paul was uncertain as to whether his imprisonment would end with his death or his release. In either case, he wanted Christ to be exalted. While he desired to be with Christ, he recognized the need to remain and continue his ministry (vv. 19-26).

The second half of this section is an appeal to the Philippians to show steadfastness and stamina in the face of opposition (vv. 27-30). They must stand as a unified family, and therefore Paul warned against selfish ambition and personal conceit (2:1-4). To demonstrate the attitude required for unity, Paul pointed to the example of Christ (vv. 5-11), possibly an early hymn/confession.

Paul called them to radical obedience accompanied by an attitude that was devoid of grumbling and disputing. Such a posture would prove them to be children of God and enable them to shine as lights in a dark world. Paul was so concerned for the growing spiritual health of the church that he would gladly pour out his life as a drink offering to nourish the faith and purity of the church.

Paul's Future Plans (2:19-30)

Paul expressed his hope that he would be released so he could visit Philippi in person (2:24). In the meantime, he planned to send Timothy, who shared his passionate concern for the welfare of the church (v. 20).

Paul also planned to send Epaphroditus, the messenger from Philippi who had brought the church's financial gift to him (v. 25). Epaphroditus had become so sick that Paul feared he would die. He had recovered by God's mercy, and now Paul wanted to send him back to Philippi so that it would relieve their concern and his. He encouraged them to receive him with joy and hold him in high regard (vv. 26-30).

Exhortations to Christian Living (3:1–4:9)

This section includes specific warnings against false teachers. Paul first warned against the legalism of Judaizers, who stressed circumcision and fleshly ordinances. Paul could compare his Jewish credentials with anyone, but he had realized that the only goal worth pursuing was a personal knowledge of Christ (3:1-16).

Paul also mentioned other troublemakers who are described as enemies of the cross of Christ. They were controlled by their earthly appetites and thus set their minds on earthly things. True believers are citizens of heaven and focus on things above (vv. 17-21).

Based on this heavenly citizenship, believers are to live in unity (4:1-3) and prayerfully rejoice in every circumstance (vv. 4-7). Those who practice such behavior will experience God's peace, which exceeds earthly understanding. Paul urged the Philippians to dwell on what is true, honorable, right, pure, lovely, things that are of good repute, and things that are worthy of praise.

Thanksgiving for God's Provision and Their Gift (4:10-23)

The Philippians had sent financial gifts to support Paul on more than one occasion. His imprisonment had provided an opportunity for them to renew their support. Paul rejoiced in their giving, not because he needed the gift, but because God would honor their generosity. His experience had taught him how to live in every circumstance knowing God would provide everything he needed (vv. 10-20).

Paul concluded in verses 21-23 with greetings from himself, the brethren with him, and saints from Caesar's household. His benediction—"The grace of the Lord Jesus Christ be with your spirit."

A Key Text to Consider (2:12-18)

I found it particularly difficult to choose a single passage for the key text because there are so many memorable ones. I have always loved Paul's personal testimony in chapter 3 where he moved from works to knowing Christ and the power of His resurrection (v. 10). Philippians 4:13 is one of my wife's favorite verses because it gave her dad the courage to live and die well. But a little note in the margin of my Bible caused me to settle on this section.

Reading every passage with an eye to its context is always important, but that is especially important in this case. Paul just concluded a section describing his own present circumstances. It is apparent that some "opponents" had used Paul's imprisonment to discourage some in Philippi, which created disunity. He called the Philippians to unity, based on the attitude revealed in Christ who did not cling to His divine status but laid it aside, becoming man and humbling himself to the status of a servant who obediently died on the cross. As a result God highly exalted Him.

Work Out Your Own Salvation (vv. 12-13)

Notice that verse 12 begins with the phrase "so then," which indicates that the directives in this section flow naturally from the preceding section in which Paul commanded them to adopt the frame of mind exhibited by Christ. The phrase translated "have this attitude" in verse 5 is an imperative that would be better translated "have this frame of mind." The central component of Jesus' frame of mind was His radical commitment to total obedience.

Paul once more picks up the issue introduced in 1:27 concerning their spiritual conduct. Simply stated, the Philippians must move on to a level of maturity that demanded they be self-reliant and self-motivated in their spiritual lives, "standing firm in one spirit, with one mind striving together for the faith of the gospel." It is easy to become dependent on a spiritual mentor in terms of our spiritual growth. Paul was calling them to become responsible for working out their own salvation.

Paul addressed them as "beloved," emphasizing his intimate relationship with the members of this church who had supported him throughout his ministry. He began by underlining their consistent attitude of obedience. Paul began with appropriate praise before he called them to a further level of commitment. His presence or lack thereof should not be the determining factor in their obedience.

Christians are each personally responsible to God and therefore must work out their own salvation. This imperative in no way suggests that persons can effect their own salvation in the sense of earning it. This is made clear by the immediate reminder in verse 13 that God is at work in us "to will and to work for His good pleasure." The basic idea is that Christians are responsible to live in regard to their salvation. In other words, they are to give it practical expression in their own lives.

To behave like Christians requires an attitude of obedience. The Philippians' obedience was not to be determined by their commitment to Paul, but to God. They must solve issues in the church as an act of obedience to God, whether or not Paul was present.

The context of such obedience is clarified by the phrase "fear and trembling" (v. 12). First, this suggests sober reverence for God. The Christian's only appropriate response is to commit to carry to conclusion, through personal effort and spiritual discipline, what God has wrought in that person's life through the sacrificial death of Christ. Second, "fear and trembling" suggests the Christian's consciousness of his or her own weakness and inability, which leads a believer to ultimate dependence upon God.

Paul then provided the reason for this command and the secret to obeying it—"for it is God who is at work in you" (v. 13). This is a clear reminder that our salvation is a work of God and not based on any merit of our own. Using a play on words we are to "work out" what God is at "work in." God's powerful in-working impacts both the will and the work, the desire and the activity. Salvation is all of God—both the will and the work—but at the same moment it requires the activity of humans. Divine sovereignty does not negate human responsibility; it demands it.

The fact that the end result is God's good pleasure is noteworthy. The idea is the ultimate glory of God (cf. Eph. 3:10). When the Philippians "work out" their salvation in terms of rejecting selfish ambition, strife, and pride—issues that could divide the church (2:3-4)—it would accomplish God's purpose and bring Him glory.

Children of God without Blemish (vv. 14-16)

These next verses are one long sentence. The command in verse 14, "Do all things without grumbling or disputing," though stated negatively, has a positive impact. It is difficult to read those words without thinking of the behavior of the Israelites as Moses led them to the promised land. Grumbling is at its very root the unwillingness to accept God's plans and appropriate His provision. Perhaps Paul had in mind the lack of humility and empathy reflected in 2:3-4.

The positive purpose of the command is made clear in verses 15-16. The Philippians were to become pure and blameless. Inner purity would be manifest in outward behavior, which would impact their witness. Paul was calling them to Christian character that would enable them to live above reproach. The language here is consistent with the thrust of his prayer in 1:9-11.

The believers' character is particularly striking when displayed and seen "in the midst of a crooked and perverse generation" (v. 15). Paul used the words of Deuteronomy 32:5b to picture the world as distorted and depraved. The world is morally crooked because of its failure to accept, understand, and apply the word of

God. The role of the Christian and the ministry of the church are to provide a pure model for a world that lives in darkness where values are distorted.

Paul's second illustration for the role of God's pure and blameless children is taken from astronomy. The function of blameless believers is to be like stars that appear as lights in the dark world. One cannot help but think of the Prologue of John's Gospel where Jesus is presented as life and light that shines in the darkness (1:4-5). Now those who are followers of Christ have the same role as the One they follow.

Believers accomplish this mission by "holding fast the word of life" (Phil. 2:16). Christians are light-spreaders, because they possess, or rather are possessed by, the word of life (John 6:63). The word of life is the gospel that leads to life. The Christian is to hold steadfast to the word of life through obedience leading to moral holiness. By becoming lights in the world, they hold out the light toward others like a torch.

Paul had a special interest in the testimony emanating from the Philippian believers' lives, since they were the fruit of his apostolic labor. Looking toward the day of Christ, they would give him reason to glory since they were the fruit of his labor (v. 16). Using athletic imagery Paul concluded that their faith and progress would demonstrate that he did not run in vain. We should not understand this as selfish motivation. Paul had already indicated that life for him was Christ (1:20-21), and thus his only concern was to please Christ and glorify Him through His labor.

For the Christian to desire to have a productive and fruitful ministry is in no way inappropriate. No one wants to run or toil in vain. Our desire in fruitful living is to hold out the word of life and thus give glory to Him who is life and light. Faithful devotion to the task given to us is our ultimate reward in the day of Christ.

Personal Joy in Ministry (vv. 17-18)

Paul then used sacrificial terminology to speak of his entire apostolic ministry. "Poured out" refers to a drink offering that accompanied the sacrifice and was poured next to or around the altar where the sacrifice was placed. "Sacrifice" was the actual offering, and together they were a service to God (v. 17).

Paul used the present tense "being poured out," suggesting something already in process. Some think Paul was speaking of his impending martyrdom, but the tone of the letter suggests he anticipated release. Most likely Paul was referring to his apostolic ministry, which often involved suffering and hardship. In chapter 1 he spoke of the privilege given to the Philippians to suffer for Christ's sake (vv. 28-29). Ministry involves the pouring out of oneself, but what better way to live than to be poured out in service to God by holding forth the word of life?

Paul reasoned, "But even if I am being poured out as a drink offering upon the sacrifice and service of your faith, I rejoice and share my joy with you all" (2:17b). Paul humbly saw himself as the drink offering around the altar, while the faith of the Philippians was the sacrifice in service to the Lord. In the ritual the drink offering was secondary, while the sacrifice was primary. Their gift that enabled his ministry and their response to his ministry was the sacrifice laid before the Lord.

Paul was in no way discouraged by his present circumstances; he had great joy. The theme of joy runs throughout this short letter. In verses 17-18 the idea occurs four times. Paul rejoiced and shared his joy with them. He then urged them to rejoice and share their joy with him. Mutual joy should be the purpose and end result of all service that brings glory to God.

For Memory and Meditation

"Holding fast the word of life, so that in the day of Christ I will have reason to glory because I did not run in vain nor toil in vain." (Phil. 2:16)

Chapter 11

1 Timothy

Focal Passage: 1 Timothy 4:6-16

The next three letters are referred to collectively as the "Pastoral Epistles" because they are directed to individuals with pastoral duties. That doesn't mean that readers who do not have pastoral duties will not profit from studying them. These letters cover a number of topics and are of great value to the church corporately and to every believer individually.

All the Pastorals are attributed to the apostle Paul. This view was held by most readers until the nineteenth century, when some scholars began to question the view based on issues such as style, vocabulary, theology, and complexity of church organization. All of these objections have been answered based on the subject matter, life experience of Paul, and the intended recipients. Internal evidence points to Paul as the author. External evidence from church history is virtually uniform in confirming Paul as the author. The best conclusion is that Paul wrote the Pastorals in the final years of his ministry through an amanuensis who was given some latitude in choice of language.

Where Was Paul? Why Did He Write 1 Timothy?

To maintain Pauline authorship of the Pastorals we must locate them in the period between Paul's release from his first Roman imprisonment and the date of his execution. Luke concluded his Acts narrative with the apostle Paul in prison "preaching the kingdom of God and teaching concerning the Lord Jesus Christ with all openness, unhindered" (28:31).

Luke indicated that Paul stayed two full years in rented quarters (v. 30), but he did not mention Paul's release or his death. The fact that Luke did not record any event after the house imprisonment does not mean that Paul's story ended at this time with his martyrdom. It is likely that Luke would have included Paul's martyrdom if it had crowned the Acts story. The declaration of Agrippa, agreed upon by Festus, that Paul had done nothing worthy of death or imprisonment would have disposed Roman officials toward a favorable trial (26:31-32). As we have seen, the Prison Epistles consistently bear witness of Paul's anticipation of impending release (Phil. 1:25; 2:23-24; Philem. 22).

If we date Paul's arrival in Rome for his first imprisonment around AD 61, we would conclude that his release occurred around AD 63, prior to the burning of Rome in AD 64. We know for certain that Paul's death occurred during Nero's reign (54–68). The most likely date of his death would be between 64 and 67, with many scholars selecting AD 66.

In 1 Timothy 1:3 Paul mentioned his departure from Ephesus for Macedonia and his instructions that Timothy remain at Ephesus to deal with men who were teaching strange doctrines. This particular trip to Macedonia does not fit in any of the three missionary journeys mentioned in Acts and therefore would support the contention that Paul wrote this letter after his release from prison.

We cannot establish with absolute certainty Paul's movements after his release. The Pastorals provide several suggestions concerning possible points of interest, and early church fathers suggest Paul fulfilled his plan to visit Spain.

A possible reconstruction begins with Paul sending Timothy to Philippi to fulfill his promise to that congregation (Phil. 2:19).

Paul himself returned east, stopping at the island of Crete where he had a successful ministry, and left Titus behind to organize and instruct the infant churches (Titus 1:5). Paul left Crete, landing at Ephesus and continuing on to Colossae for the promised visit with Philemon (Philem. 22). He then returned to Ephesus where he was joined by Timothy.

Paul discovered that the church was facing several issues, including false teachers, so he left Timothy to deal with these issues (1 Tim. 1:3-4). When Paul departed from Ephesus, he traveled to Philippi as planned (Phil. 2:24). He hoped to return quickly to Ephesus but feared that his return would be delayed (1 Tim. 3:14-15) and therefore wrote two letters, 1 Timothy (cf. 1 Tim. 1:3) and Titus, which are similar in content and style, around AD 63 or 64.[1]

By reading 1 Timothy, we find several statements that suggest that Paul intended the letter to be read both by Timothy and the church at large. In chapter one he addressed Timothy directly to encourage him to stand firm against men who teach strange doctrines. To fortify him, Paul reminded him of the gift for ministry he had received (4:14), his "good confession" (6:12), and the gospel that had been entrusted to him (v. 20). Paul's concluding greeting in verse 21 is plural, a further indication of a larger audience. A word from the apostle to the church would certainly assist Timothy in dealing with the heretics and organizing the church.

To assist Timothy in standing against heresy, Paul included information that would help him identity the false teachers and the nature of their teaching. The false teachers had legalistic tendencies and urged dietary restrictions and asceticism (1:7-8; 4:3). They claimed a higher knowledge based on a type of mysticism (6:20-21).

For the ongoing strength and stability of the church, Paul provided detailed directions for proper conduct for public worship (ch. 2). High standards were established for those who would speak in the assembly or provide any leadership for the local church.

An Overview of the Letter

Paul's salutation in verses 1 and 2 follows his usual pattern, identifying himself as the author and Timothy as the recipient. He addressed Timothy as his "true child," indicating the close relationship of mentor and mentee.

Timothy's Task (1:3-20)

Paul charged Timothy with preventing the spread of false teaching by contrasting the gospel and its counterfeits (vv. 3-11). He used his own story to emphasize the importance of preaching the gospel (vv. 12-17). Paul concluded this section in verses 18-20 with a charge to Timothy to fight the good fight by keeping faith and a good conscience.

Worship and Order in the Church (2:1–4:16)

This is the longest section of the letter because stability in the church is the greatest deterrent to false teaching. Paul began with an emphasis on prayer for all people and particularly for those in positions of leadership (2:1-7). He then called both men and women to prayer and holy living (v. 8). Men were to renounce their inclination toward wrath and dissension. Women were to produce good works, focus on learning before leading, and practice mothering with love and self-restraint (vv. 9-15).

Chapter 3 contains the qualifications Paul laid out for overseers, deacons, and women who assist in ministry (vv. 1-13).

Since strong-willed leaders had caused problems in Ephesus, Paul wanted to ensure that future leaders would possess qualifications that strongly emphasize character. Some of the observable traits mentioned are obedient behavior, leadership in the home, spiritual maturity, and respect among those outside the church.

Verses 14-16 seem to have wider application to all readers concerning how to conduct oneself in the household of God. Christians are to see themselves as God's family and live consistently based on that high calling.

In chapter 4 Paul spoke to the heresy that included ascetic practices, forbidding marriage, and the eating of certain foods. He insisted that all of God's creation is good and should be received with gratitude (vv. 1-5). To deal with the false teachers, Timothy must be nourished by words of faith and sound doctrine and avoid worldly fables. He was to fix his hope on the living God, give attention to public reading of Scripture, not neglect the spiritual gift within him, and practice the spiritual disciplines (vv. 6-10).

Responsibilities toward Various Groups in the Church (5:1–6:2)

Paul mentioned men, women, young and old, widows, leaders, and slaves in this section, indicating something of the diversity of the early church. All of these are to be treated as family.

Paul focused first on widows (5:3-16), insisting that genuine widows deserve both financial assistance and appropriate honor. He provided careful criteria for widows who qualify. He gave special attention to the needs facing younger widows, particularly in regard to sexual temptation. He suggested that they not be put on the list for financial assistance, but he encouraged them to remarry.

The second group to be singled out is the elders who rule well by working hard at preaching and teaching (vv. 17-25). They are to be given double honor, which likely means adequate pay since it is illustrated by the ox eating from that which he is threshing. Elders are protected from frivolous complaints, but those who persist in sin are to be censured by the congregation as a deterrent to others. Paul concluded the section by providing slaves with acceptable behavior in the context of Christian and non-Christian masters (6:1-2).

Final Admonitions (6:3-21)

Paul focused once again on the behavior of the false teachers, exposing their conceit and greed. The greedy desires of the false teachers allowed Paul to speak of the dangers of the love of money (vv. 3-10).

Paul challenged Timothy to "fight the good fight of faith" (v. 12). He charged him to "keep the commandment without stain or reproach" (v. 14), which involves completing the ministry assigned to him in Ephesus. He encouraged him to instruct those rich in the present world to fix their hope on God and to do good, being ready to share (vv. 17-19). He included a final word of caution instructing Timothy to stay faithful to the task entrusted to him (vv. 20-21).

A Key Text to Consider (4:6-16)

Our key text deals with the discipline necessary for a minister of the gospel and was written uniquely to Timothy, but the advice is valuable to any and every Christian since we are all gifted for and called to ministry.

The context is about apostasy, an issue that always threatens the vitality of the church. In the case of Ephesus, the heresy manifested itself in terms of legalism and asceticism. False teachers were forbidding marriage and requiring abstinence from certain foods. The antidote was sound doctrine and authentic spiritual growth.

Be Constantly Nourished by Sound Doctrine (vv. 6-7a)

Since the church will always face the threat of false teaching, those in ministry must be able to recognize and point it out to persons in their care. "These things" (v. 6) specifically refers back to the false teaching mentioned in verses 1-5, but the antidote described here would apply equally to any form of false teaching.

"Pointing out" would not only mean describing the content of the erroneous teaching but offering positive correction. Providing such corrective teaching is evidence that one is a "good servant of Christ Jesus." The "good servant" must be "constantly nourished on the words of the faith and of sound doctrine." The present participle is used to emphasize the continual process of being nourished.

The use of the article "the" before "faith" implies the whole body of Christian doctrine, which is then explained further by the phrase "sound doctrine." There exists no better means of nourishing one's spiritual life than constant attention to the great truths of the faith. It is possible that the apostle may have had in mind specific summaries of doctrine, such as those marked by the phrase "trustworthy statement" in the Pastorals (cf. 1 Tim. 1:15; 4:9; Titus 1:9). Timothy had been privileged to learn sound doctrine at Paul's feet. Paul affirmed that Timothy had followed these truths as his standard, and now he challenged Timothy to continue to chart this course for his own life in order to be effective in nourishing others.

By way of contrast to "sound doctrine," Paul warned of "worldly fables fit only for old women" (v. 7a). The Greek word translated "fables" is *muthoi* from which we get the English word "myth." Paul was likely referring to the "myths and endless genealogies" already mentioned in 1:4. He had no intention of negatively characterizing older women; he was simply using a phrase that had a touch of irony to describe the emptiness of false doctrine. Paul had high regard for all persons, including older women, who were to be treated as honored mothers (1 Tim. 5:1-2), but he had a passionate disregard for all persons who distort and teach false doctrine. He was not disparaging men or women, but the foolishness of the doctrine.

Be Disciplined for Godliness (vv. 7b-10)

Paul moved from the image of physical and spiritual nourishment to that of physical and spiritual exercise. He may have turned to the image of athletics to provide a contrast between physical exercise and the telling of old wives tales. Timothy was to discipline or exercise himself with the end result of godliness.

Paul acknowledged that bodily exercise had some value, but it was limited in comparison with the value of training oneself for godliness. The contrast between "little profit" and "all things" is quite clear. Physical exercise could give the participant health and a better quality of earthly life, but godliness provides for spiritual health that impacts both the present and eternal future.

With our present-day sedentary lifestyle and abundance of high-calorie fast food options, a diet and exercise program is an important aspect of Christian stewardship.[2] However, in some circles, physical fitness and a healthy lifestyle have become the virtual religion. The amount of money and time spent on one's physical development greatly exceeds that which the average Christian spends developing his or her spiritual health. Does the time you spend on spiritual discipline for godliness equal or exceed the time you spend eating and exercising?

Verse 9 contains the second of two "trustworthy statement" sayings in this letter. (The first is found in 1:15 concerning the coming of Jesus into the world to save sinners.) This phrase seems to suggest a well-known saying that was accepted by all believers. In this instance there is disagreement as to whether the phrase refers to the preceding verse or the one following. Verse 8 sounds more like a proverbial saying, but verse 10 contains weightier theological content.

In either case, Paul's point is clear. Given the eternal value of godliness, we labor and strive because our focus and hope is on the living God. The race for godliness demands that we use every ounce of strength available to us. Paul and Timothy strove in the spiritual arena of life where the battle is against spiritual forces of darkness. They gladly did so because they had fixed their hope steadfastly on the living God. The perfect tense indicates a continuous state of hope. We know that we have life to come because our hope is in the "living God" (vv. 8, 10).

"The living God . . . is the Savior of all men, especially of believers." This phrase clearly cannot refer to every person living on earth (universalism) because of the clear teaching of Scripture. It is best to understand "Savior" in the familiar Old Testament meaning of "Preserver" or "Deliverer." It speaks to God's universal love and provision for all humanity. God's love extends to all, and His offer of redemption is available to all. However, He is the Savior, in the special sense of "Redeemer" for those who by faith embrace Him and fix their hope upon Him for eternal life.

Be Exemplary in Your Behavior (vv. 11-12)

Faithful ministers must prescribe, teach, and show. While these admonitions are directed specifically to Timothy, they apply to anyone who desires to be effective in ministry. In verse 11, "prescribe" means "command"; and both this word and "teach" are present imperatives, meaning Timothy must continually and consistently command and teach. The content of his teaching was sound doctrine and of such value that he was called to teach with the authority consistent with his content.

Paul was aware that Timothy's relative youth might cause him to be hesitant about preaching and teaching with authority. His authority was not in his age but in his calling and his content. Certainly, he was ministering to persons older than himself.

Timothy was to counteract the possible negative response to his age by exemplary behavior. Paul mentioned speech, conduct, love, faith, and purity (v. 12); the first two apply to public life and the other three to inner qualities, but even these will have a public manifestation. "Speech" here is conversation rather than preaching, which has already been covered. In other words, Timothy's life must correspond to the sound doctrine he commands in his preaching.

Be Absorbed in These Things (vv. 13-16)

These directions are not to be taken lightly; Timothy was to "take pains with these things" (v. 15). "Until I come" in verse 13 harmonizes with Paul's desire and plans stated in 3:14. The three pursuits mentioned in this verse are related to Timothy's public ministry. "Reading" is generally understood as the reading aloud of Scripture. As in the synagogue, the reading of Scripture was followed by an exhortation (warning, advice, or encouragement) based on the Scripture. In early Christian worship "teaching," which means doctrinal instruction, was given a special place. Paul was not giving a complete description of the worship service; but he was giving Timothy personal advice about those things that must be kept in balance.

Timothy had been gifted by God, affirmed through prophetic utterance, and confirmed by the church leaders. The gift (*charismata*) is the spiritual gifting that comes through the ministry of the Holy Spirit.[3] God always gifts His people to accomplish that which He has created and called them to do.

The gifting of Timothy was confirmed through prophecy (cf. 1 Tim. 1:18). Confirmation through prophecy likely refers to the sense of assurance God granted Paul concerning the calling and gifting of this young man. We see a similar prophetic confirmation issued by the church at Antioch regarding Paul and Barnabas before the church laid hands on them and sent them on the first missionary journey (Acts 13:1-3).

Finally, Timothy's call to ministry was confirmed by the church leaders who, as a sign of their confidence, laid their hands on him. The idea of imparting a spiritual gift through the laying on of hands is frequently found in the Acts narrative (8:17; 9:17; 19:6). The laying on of hands symbolizes the transfer of a gift and provides a beautiful picture of the balance between sovereign calling and human participation.

Paul's instructions to Timothy were to be of such priority that he used two phrases to suggest maximum effort: "Take pains in these things, be absorbed in them" (1 Tim. 4:15). The first phrase suggests they must constantly be in Timothy's mind. The second phrase literally means to "be in them." They are like Timothy's oxygen, and to survive he must be immersed in them. So intense must be his effort that his progress will be evident to everyone.

Paul's final admonition linked teacher and teaching in an indissoluble union. First, Timothy must keep an eye on himself. When a teacher fails to embrace his own teaching, when orthodoxy is not accompanied by orthopraxy, there is a risk that the listeners will see the hypocrisy and dismiss the teacher and his teaching. But when the two are companions, the power inherent in the teaching "will ensure the salvation both for yourself and for those who hear you" (v. 16).

We are all saved by grace and not by works, and thus Paul was not suggesting that Timothy would earn his salvation. Timothy would be working out his salvation in the sense we saw in Philippians 2:12, and at the same time he would assist those under his care in doing the same.

For Memory and Meditation

"For bodily discipline is only of little profit, but godliness is profitable for all things, since it holds promise for the present life and also for the life to come." (1 Tim. 4:8)

---

[1] This reconstruction of Paul's travels closely follows William Hendricks, *I-II Timothy and Titus* (Grand Rapids, MI: Baker Book House, 1957), 40.

[2] If you are interested in a study on fitness that looks at a biblical pattern for total wellness see my book, *Well2Serve* (Tigerville, SC: Auxano Press, 2014).

[3] To study more about spiritual gifts, consider the twelve-week DVD study *You Are Gifted*, available through Auxanopress.com.

Chapter 12

Titus

Focal Passage: Titus 2:1-14

Titus was perhaps one of the least noticed yet most vital members of Paul's missionary team. He is not mentioned in Acts, but he makes several appearances in Paul's letters. Titus was frequently mentioned by Paul in his letters and was the recipient of the letter that bears his name.

The greeting "my true child in a common faith" (1:4) certainly indicates a close relationship between Paul and Titus and may suggest that Paul was responsible for leading him to embrace Christ as Savior. We first meet Titus in Galatians 2:1-5, which chronicles a critical moment in the life of Paul and in early church history.

Paul's fruitful ministry among the Gentiles had created tension as to whether the early church would endorse his work and his practice of baptizing Gentile believers without requiring them to become Jews first through circumcision and pay attention to Jewish rituals. When Paul first journeyed to Jerusalem to plead his case concerning his ministry to the Gentiles, he was accompanied by Barnabas and Titus (Gal. 2:1). It is likely that Titus was Paul's prime example of a Gentile convert. He rejoiced that Titus, even though a Greek, was not required to be circumcised (v. 3). The mention in Galatians 2 may indicate Titus was known to the Galatians, possibly from the first missionary journey to that region.

Clearly Titus became one of Paul's most trusted partners (2 Cor. 8:23) and therefore was given tremendous responsibility in dealing with a very troubled and difficult congregation in Corinth. It is challenging to determine exactly how many trips Titus made to Corinth, but it is apparent that he was both needed and effective.

Titus was assigned the unenviable task of personally delivering the tearful letter (2 Cor. 2:1-4) and addressing personally the critical issues in the church. The Corinthians apparently responded well to Titus, and his successful report comforted Paul (7:13-16). Titus's evenhanded and compassionate care for the Corinthians greatly endeared him to the church and to Paul (8:16-17; 12:18). Paul, now in Macedonia, had been anxiously waiting for Titus's report (2:13; 7:5-6). Hearing the good news, Paul quickly responded by writing 2 Corinthians and likely had Titus deliver the letter in person (8:6, 16-18). Titus was given the additional responsibility of being one of the messengers who would deliver the offering for the saints in Jerusalem (8:23).

After Paul's imprisonment in Rome, and nearing the end of his great missionary career, he wrote a personal letter to Titus, who was on special assignment in Crete (Titus 1:5). As Paul concluded the letter, he requested that Titus meet him in Nicopolis, where he was spending the winter (3:12). After Paul was imprisoned in Rome for a second time, Titus was sent to Dalmatia (2 Tim. 4:10).

Where Was Paul? Why Did He Write Titus?

After Paul left Timothy in Ephesus, he returned to Macedonia as planned (Phil. 2:24; 1 Tim. 1:3). After he wrote his first letter to Timothy, Paul soon thereafter composed the letter to Titus, who had been left in Crete to establish order in that church.

The moral reputation of the Cretans was not excellent, a point at least one of their prophets confirmed (Titus 1:12-13). The Cretans needed well-qualified leaders to speak to moral issues and stand against the false teachers. You will notice a strong emphasis on godly living throughout the letter. Paul insisted that believers must be taught to abstain from worldly lusts and to live moderately and righteously. Those who continued to cause trouble to believers must be strongly disciplined.

The letter itself suggests that Paul had several purposes in mind as he was moved by the Spirit to pen this letter to Titus. First, he wanted to provide clear directions for establishing mature ongoing leadership for the congregation. This would have the long-term impact of helping the congregation recognize and stand against false teachers. Second, he wanted to provide directions for establishing a spirit of sanctification in congregational, personal, family, and social relationships. Third, he wanted the church to assist in the support of Zenas and Apollos. Finally, he wanted to urge Titus to join him in Nicopolis for the winter when a suitable substitute could take over his work in Crete.

An Overview of the Letter

Salutation (1:1-4)

The salutation follows the general form of Paul's other letters. It does, however, differ slightly in that it includes a fairly lengthy section describing the scope and nature of God's redemptive plan, mentioning Paul's unique role in proclaiming God's message of eternal life. Paul's personal greeting is similar to that used for Timothy.

Directions for Selecting Church Leaders (1:5-16)

The selection of leaders is of utmost importance since these leaders would provide ongoing instruction of the church and protection against false teachers (vv. 5-9). The false teachers are described as rebellious, empty talkers, and deceivers. Some were emphasizing Jewish legalism and were upsetting entire families. Driven by greed, they had spread their errors widely. They professed to know God but denied Him by their behavior (vv. 10-16).

Regulations and Basis for Christian Behavior (2:1-15)

Paul instructed Titus to pay particular attention to five different groups of persons as he taught them sound doctrine. He was to urge the older men to persevere in temperate, dignified, and sensible faith (v. 2). The older women were to be good examples in character and behavior in order to encourage the young women to love their husbands and children, establishing a healthy home (vv. 3-5). The young men were called to be sensible, pure in doctrine, sound in speech, and beyond reproach. Slaves were to be obedient to masters and above reproach in their behavior.

All these relationships are presented with a view of their impact on the gospel. The phrases "so that the word of God will not be dishonored" in verse 5; "so that the opponent will be put to shame, having nothing bad to say about us" in verse 8; and "so that they will adorn the doctrine of God our Savior in every respect" in verse 10 remind us that Christian behavior is integral to the spread of the gospel.

Paul established three factors that should motivate one to committed Christian living. First is the grace of God, which brought the possibility of salvation to all persons (v. 11). Second, the blessed hope of Christ's imminent return demands that we live righteously in the present age (vv. 12-13). Third, the solemn recognition that we are God's own possession mandates zeal for good deeds (v. 14). Titus has the full authority of God to speak these things, and he should not be disregarded (v. 15).

The Theological Basis for Christian Living (3:1-11)

Paul began this section with an emphasis on proper relationship to governmental authorities and considerate conduct toward all people (vv. 1-2). There are two overarching reasons mandating that Christians live such a radical lifestyle. First, we must be reminded what our lives were like before we experienced God's kindness (vv. 3-4). Second, we have been renewed by the Holy Spirit, who empowers us for new life (vv. 5-7).

Paul concluded this section by the affirmation, "This is a trustworthy statement," and thus Titus could speak boldly in challenging all believers to engage in good deeds. Titus must avoid empty discussions about insignificant issues that were worthless (vv. 8-9). If false teachers persisted after being warned, they were to be rejected (vv. 10-11).

Personal Concerns and Greetings (3:12-15)

Paul spoke of his intention to send Artemas or Tychicus to replace Titus so that he could spend the winter with him in Nicopolis. Further, he encouraged Titus to provide assistance to Zenas and Apollos, Christian workers who were presently in Crete. It is possible they were the couriers of this letter.

A Key Text to Consider (2:1-14)

In chapter 1 Paul gave instructions to enable Titus to complete the organization of the churches on the island of Crete. These qualified leaders would be able to provide sound doctrinal instruction so that false teachers would be silenced. Paul's final indictment of the false teachers was that their profession and behavior did not match, and thus they were worthless for any good deed (v. 15).

Paul then focused his attention on sound doctrine as it relates to the family and the individual.

Sound Doctrine and Older Believers (vv. 1-3)

The linking phrase "but as for you" draws an intentional contrast between the ministry of Titus and that of the false teachers. The false teachers were guilty of empty words, and thus Titus must speak words that were suitable for sound doctrine. The importance of sound doctrine was introduced in 1:9 and its need reinforced in 1:13. The church would either suffer the disease of heresy or maintain sound health through doctrinal training.

The word "speak" in 2:1 translates a simple Greek term that would include normal conversation. It is not enough that church leaders formally teach sound doctrine; it must be the topic of their daily conversation. In contrast to the false teachers, the lives of those who lead must fully harmonize with the doctrine they espouse.

Paul began with the older men and women, since the senior members of the community must prove to be examples for younger members of the congregation. Their life experience should give them wisdom to sort out the difference between that which is of eternal value and that which is vacuous.

The first three qualities listed for the men might well be said of anyone who has attained maturity, but they have special meaning for the believer. Older men must be "temperate," a word primarily meaning sobriety in contrast to drunkenness. Here, however, it suggests moderation in all of life. Mature men should have sufficient life experience and exposure to God's Word that they have discovered a meaningful life is lived in correspondence with God's purpose. It is sad when older Christian men suffer a spiritual midlife crisis and chase ephemeral goals that demonstrate a lack of temperance.

Further, older men must be dignified, which means serious and respectable. Being respectable does not mean being dull and boring, which would turn people from the gospel. These men must exhibit sound judgment and proper restraint. "Sensible" speaks of the individual whose actions correspond with their sound judgment. Spiritual maturation means that we are continually narrowing the gap between conviction and behavior.

The next triad is distinctively Christian—"sound in faith, in love, in perseverance." The linking of these three virtues is also found in one of Paul's earliest letters (1 Th. 1:3) as well as the other two pastoral letters (1 Tim. 6:11-12; 2 Tim. 3:10). As we read the Pastorals in conjunction with one another, it becomes clear that the qualifications for pastors and deacons, and those for all members of the church, are very similar.

"Faith" here probably means the ability to trust God. Surely those who have walked longer in the faith should have a greater capacity to trust God with the daily affairs of life. Growth in love would suggest a greater desire and capacity to work for the best interests of others. "Perseverance" is not a spirit of resignation in the face of difficulties but a positive view of God that enables us to transform hardships into learning opportunities.

The use of the word "sound" here with "faith" is not insignificant; it is the same word used in verse one to describe the teaching Titus must embrace and speak. This suggests that "sound behavior" should flow from "sound doctrine."

Paul began his instructions related to older women with the word "likewise," indicating the similarities of the requirements for older women. The English phrase "reverent in their behavior" translates two Greek words that are unique in the New Testament.

Widespread agreement exists among commentators that the language suggests a priestess carrying out her duties. The idea is that older women are to carry into daily life the demeanor of priestesses in a temple. The two prohibitions that follow, "not malicious gossips nor enslaved to much wine," vividly portray the Cretan environment (cf. 1:12) and the contrast between the saved and unsaved.

Goals for Young Women and Men (vv. 4-8)

Instead of using their tongues for malicious gossip, older women are to focus on "teaching what is good" (v. 3). The final phrase of verse 3 is linked closely to verses 4 and 5 by the phrase "so that." The teaching by word and deed of the older women has the unique goal of encouraging young women to love their husbands and children. Older women have the experience necessary to help young women deal with the challenges of family life, an issue especially important in Crete, since the false teachers had upset whole families (1:11).

The word "sensible" is the same quality required of older men in verse 2. In both cases it means self-control, but here it is particularized with the addition of "pure," which means one who is free from sin (cf. 1 Tim. 5:22). "Workers at home" suggests the sphere of a woman's primary spiritual responsibility and underlines the effort required in running a household. Kindness is a virtue that can be lacking in the midst of the daily strain of managing a home.

A woman's equal standing before God (Gal. 3:28) does not negate God's order for the home. In Ephesians 5:22-33 Paul made it abundantly clear that the husband is to love his wife as Christ loved the church. Proper order is not an issue in a Christian home when a husband practices self-giving love.

Attention to behavior, especially in the home, has a uniquely evangelistic goal for the believer "so that the word of God will not be dishonored." The use of "word" suggests that behavior that did not meet the high standard of the gospel would, in fact, be a denial of the gospel.

In verse 6, Paul instructed Titus to urge the young men to be sensible, showing self-control. It seems likely that verses 7 and 8 are directed to Titus, but they are certainly applicable to the young men. Since Titus was a young man himself, it would be logical to think that Paul would urge him to be an example to those in his age group. The Greek word is *tupos*, which means the imprint from a die. It reminds us that our lives will make an impression on others.

Paul mentioned specifically good deeds, doctrine, dignity, and speech. It bears mention that action precedes teaching; the one preparing the way for the other. "Purity in doctrine" offers a strong contrast to the false teachers both in terms of their motives (1:11, "sordid gain") and their content. "Dignified" has already been used in verse 2 to describe the behavior of older men. "Sound in speech" means speech that is so pure and wholesome that it is beyond reproach, giving opponents no grounds for attack. By his life and teaching Titus would put the false teachers to shame. Christians should never give opponents legitimate ammunition to use against them.

Behavior that Adorns the Doctrine of God (vv. 9-10)

We have already seen in our study of Philemon that Paul sowed the seeds that would one day destroy completely the institution of slavery. But, knowing the present circumstances in Crete, Paul gave directions to slaves that would enable them to live in such a manner that they would visualize the gospel for their masters.

The instructions are basic—requiring obedience, hard work, integrity, and a good attitude. This behavior could be challenging if the master of the slave was an unreasonable non-Christian. The word translated "adorn" is *kosmeo*, from which we derive the English word "cosmetic." It was used of the arrangement of jewels in a manner to show their full beauty. By living out a radical Christian ethic in a negative environment, the slave had the opportunity to make the doctrine of God look beautiful in the eyes of all men.

The Theological Basis for Christian Living in Family (vv. 11-14)

Paul closed this section with his second brief theological summary in this short letter. The first was in the introduction of the letter (1:1-4), which established the doctrinal basis of truth. The third will come in 3:3-7 and establish the doctrinal basis for godly living in regard to government and all men. The consistent connection of behavior and theology suggests that all life-changing practical advice must be anchored in the truths of the Christian faith.

The theological basis for Christian living is grounded first in the Incarnation. When Christ took upon Himself human flesh, the grace of God became visible. John similarly speaks of the Incarnation in terms of the glory of God manifesting itself in human flesh, "full of grace and truth" (John 1:14). This grace brought salvation to "all men." The emphasis on "all men" in this context indicates that the atonement is unlimited, available to old and young, male and female, and even to slaves. It is available to all but must be appropriated by faith.[1]

Grace is personified as educating us in the art of Christian living. Godly living is described both negatively and positively. We must first deny "ungodliness and worldly desires" (v. 12). "Ungodliness" would mean to live as if God did not exist. "Worldly desires" refers to desires that are entirely centered in the present world system. Without denying these first, it is impossible to "live sensibly, righteously and godly."

Verse 12 closes with a reference to the present age, but verse 13 makes clear that believers live in the present age based on our hope for the future. For the believer "the blessed hope" is not something in question but that which is assured. The content of our hope is the sure return of "our great God and Savior, Christ Jesus." The reference to Christ Jesus as God and Savior is a strong affirmation of His full deity.

Paul continued in verse 14 by focusing on Christ's self-giving act of redemption. It appears that the wording may have been taken from Psalm 130:8, which says, "And He will redeem Israel / From all his iniquities." Christ gave Himself to purchase us at the cost of His own life. He bought us out of the debt caused by our lawlessness. He not only redeems us; He purifies us so that we can be "His own possession, zealous for good deeds." The phrase "His own possession" harks back to a pivotal Old Testament promise where redeemed Israel was called "My own possession" (Ex. 19:5).

The three forces that motivate us to live godly lives are: the grace of God experienced in salvation, the blessed hope assured in Christ's return, and His redemption and sanctification enabling us to be His own possession.

For Memory and Meditation

"In all things show yourself to be an example of good deeds, with purity in doctrine, dignified." (Titus 2:7)

---

[1] For a study of the extent of the atonement, see my six-week study, *Unlimited: God's Love, Atonement, and Mission* (Travelers Rest, SC: Auxano Press, 2018).

Chapter 13

2 Timothy

Focal Passage: 2 Timothy 1:3-14

The last letter we possess from the hand of Paul is 2 Timothy. It could have been written within weeks or days of his martyrdom. It has the sound and feel of a last will and testament. In earlier letters from his house imprisonment, Paul expressed both his desire and hope for future ministry. This letter contains a word of finality—"For I am already being poured out as a drink offering, and the time of my departure has come. I have fought the good fight, I have finished the course, I have kept the faith" (4:6-7).

Life must look different when you know you are facing eternity. Those who know they are approaching death often have final messages they feel compelled to convey. Last words take on extra significance. When we study 2 Timothy, we are reading the last words of the greatest church planter of all time.

Where Was Paul? Why Did He Write 2 Timothy?

In our study of 1 Timothy and Titus we noticed that the tone of the letters spoke of future travel and ministry. In 2 Timothy Paul wrote as a prisoner anticipating death. Where has Paul been since his release from the first imprisonment until now? The final places mentioned in the previous two pastoral letters were Crete (Titus 1:5), Ephesus (1 Tim. 1:3), Macedonia (1 Tim. 1:3), and Nicopolis (Titus 3:12). No one knows for certain if Paul actually journeyed to these places in this order, but the route is rather direct and thus makes sense. The final places mentioned in 2 Timothy are Miletus, Troas, and Corinth.

Possibly a mission to Spain intervened between the two routes of travel the Pastorals suggest. Let's pick up the story upon Paul's return from Spain. Based on the places mentioned in 2 Timothy, Paul traveled to Asia Minor and left Trophimus, who was ill, at Miletus (4:20). At Troas he visited Carpus and inadvertently left his cloak (v. 13). His final stop before Rome would have been Corinth, where he left Erastus (v. 20).

From Corinth he traveled to Rome, perhaps to report to the church that had sponsored his mission work to Spain. Once in Rome, he was arrested again. (It is also possible he was arrested and taken to Rome). This was no house arrest with relative freedom as had been the case a few years prior. His imprisonment was short and cruel (1:16-17; 2:9).

Nero, the cruel emperor who murdered his own stepbrother, his mother, his wife Octavia, his tutor (Seneca), and many others, was in power. When Rome burned in AD 64, the people accused Nero of setting the fire; and Nero attempted to deflect the blame to the Christians. The carnage in terms of human life was frightful, and Paul may well have been one among many believers to be sacrificed by the madman.

The winter mentioned in Titus 3:12 that Paul planned to spend in Nicopolis as a free man and the winter mentioned in 2 Timothy 4:21 were not the same. In the latter he was a prisoner asking for Timothy to bring Mark with him along with his cloak and books (vv. 11-13). We can suggest this letter was written by Paul from Roman imprisonment in AD 65 or 66, just before he was beheaded on the Ostian Way about three miles outside the capital. We do not know if Timothy and Mark arrived in time to be with the apostle before His death.[1]

Likely, Timothy was still in Ephesus when he received this second letter. Paul had undergone a preliminary hearing (4:16) and fully anticipated that he would die soon (vv. 6-8). A few believers had ministered to Paul at great risk (1:16-18), but others had deserted him (4:14-16). Some of his friends had left on specific ministry assignments (vv. 10b-12); and, other than Luke, Paul was alone.

Paul wrote this letter as a personal exhortation and encouragement to his young protégé. The false teachers in Ephesus continued to trouble the church. Hymenaeus, who had been excommunicated earlier (1 Tim. 1:20) was still causing trouble and apparently had recruited others to join him. Their teaching was spreading like gangrene (2 Tim. 2:17-18). Paul wanted to assist Timothy in dealing with the heresy, but his real goal was to encourage Timothy by affirming his qualifications and preparation for handling any situation.

Paul encouraged Timothy to be loyal to his teaching and practice (1:13-14; 2:1-13). To prepare the church for long-term health, Timothy was to focus on developing faithful followers of Christ who would in turn develop others (2:1-2). Finally, he urged Timothy to come to visit him as soon as possible. It is not surprising that the great warrior wanted his true son in the faith by his side in his final days.

An Overview of the Letter

The salutation is standard and brief (1:1-2). Interestingly, the threefold blessing of grace, mercy, and peace is the same as in 1 Timothy, but it is not repeated in any of Paul's other letters.

Encouraging Words Based on Experience (1:3-18)

Paul expressed heartfelt gratitude for Timothy's faithful ministry. He recalled Timothy's heritage from his grandmother and mother and challenged him to "kindle afresh the gift of God" in him (v. 6). He spoke of his own suffering to prepare Timothy for the possibility that he, too, would suffer (vv. 8-12). Timothy would endure by retaining sound doctrine and guarding the treasure entrusted to him. Paul mentioned briefly those who turned away from him and then focused on Onesiphorus who was a positive example for Timothy (vv. 15-18).

Directions to Timothy (2:1-26)

Paul's challenge to his young protégé was moving and personal. He urged Timothy to select leaders who would receive and transmit the truths he had learned from Paul. He used the images of a soldier, an athlete, and a farmer to describe the work of the effective minister (vv. 3-7). In verses 8-13 Paul returned to the bottom line of ministry, which is the risen Christ and the unfettered word. The trustworthy statement (vv. 11-13) may be a remnant of an early hymn that gave assurance that believers would reign with Christ.

Paul encouraged Timothy to take the lead in opposing falsehood by warning of its danger and exposing its errors. To do so, he must be diligent in the handling of God's Word and avoid worldly and empty chatter (vv. 14-19). Timothy must be a clean vessel, useful to the Master, by fleeing youthful lusts and pursuing righteousness (vv. 20-22). No value would be gained by joining in the contentious debates, and thus Timothy must be able to teach, be patient when wronged, and be gentle when correcting (vv. 23-26).

The Stubborn Character of False Teachers (3:1-9)

Paul wanted Timothy to understand the nature of those who oppose the truth. He described them as self-centered, greedy, arrogant, ungrateful, unholy, unloving, irreconcilable, and the list continues. They had a form of godliness but denied its power. They preyed on the weak and gullible.

The Man of God Is Adequate and Equipped (3:10-17)

Timothy may have feared that he would not be able to stand up under the constant bombardment of these false teachers. Paul pointed again to his own ministry as an example of one who persevered (vv. 10-11). Since persecution will be experienced by all who desire to live godly lives, Timothy must continue in the things he had learned from childhood and have absolute confidence in the authority and power of the Scripture (vv. 14-17).

Paul's Farewell Message (4:1-22)

The solemnity of this message gives this section the emotional impact of a last will and testament. The charge to preach the Word at all times and with sound conviction is based once again on the presence of heretical teachers. Timothy must remain balanced, endure hardship, and do the work of an evangelist (vv. 1-5).

Paul became more personal about his impending death—"I have fought the good fight, I have finished the course, I have kept the faith" (v. 7). He spoke expectantly of the crown of righteousness he would receive from the righteous Judge (v. 8).

Timothy was to pick up Mark and bring Paul's cloak and books, especially the parchments, and come to him before winter, if possible (vv. 11, 13, 21). Even though Paul had been deserted, he could celebrate that he was allowed to have a successful ministry to the Gentiles. He anticipated his final rescue when he would be brought to the heavenly kingdom. Paul concluded with personal greetings to his faithful friends and sent greetings to Timothy from other believers. His final words—"The Lord be with your spirit. Grace be with you" (vv. 19-22).

A Key Text to Consider (1:3-14)

The introductory section gives us a very personal look at the apostle and his young protégé. It is a tender and meaningful "passing of the torch."

Filled with Joy (1:3-5)

Sitting in a cold dungeon under a death sentence, Paul meditated on his many blessings, past and present. He began with sincere thanks to God for the privilege of serving Him and, in that context, having met Timothy.

Paul had carried out his service with a "clear conscience" (1:3; cf. 1 Tim. 1:5), which indicates that he served without any ulterior motives. His mind and purpose were controlled by His love of God and desire to serve Him. The mention of his "forefathers" indicates that Paul saw his response to God as a natural continuation of his Jewish worship and devotion. Although Paul saw Christianity as clearly fulfilling and superseding Jewish law, he would never speak disrespectfully of his Jewish heritage. This reference to heritage also prepares the way for what Paul intended to say about Timothy's lineage (v. 5).

Whenever Paul remembered Timothy in his prayers, he was filled with gratitude. Anyone who reads the Pauline letters will be impressed by his commitment to pray with constancy for all of the Christian communities he served. It follows that he would be equally as diligent in praying for his close associates. The phrase "night and day" in verse 3 stresses continuity and gives added emphasis to the fervency of Paul's prayers. He knew both the value and power of prayer for fruitful ministry.

Paul's constant prayers naturally led to an intense desire to see Timothy (v. 4). His desire was intensified as he remembered Timothy's tears at their last parting. It is possible that this parting is the event described in 1 Timothy 1:3 as Paul left Timothy in Ephesus to depart for Macedonia. The word "urged" in that verse may even suggest that Timothy was reluctant to remain without the great apostle. Confronting the false teachers would have a frightening prospect, made more challenging by the absence of his mentor. It is also possible that this is a reference to a later parting that would have occurred after Paul's trip to Spain.

If Paul was able to see Timothy again he would be "filled with joy." Paul was self-assured and emotionally and physically strong. He had endured every form of hardship without quitting or complaining. It is noteworthy that this strong man needed his friends and openly expressed his love for them. None of us are intended to serve alone.

Many commentators believe that the phrase "for I am mindful" (v. 5) indicates that Paul had just received news from Timothy either by letter or through a visitor. It is striking that four different expressions are used to speak of memory in verses 3-6. It is clear that prison and a likely death sentence had caused Paul to spend time reminiscing.

The thought of Timothy's service led the apostle to remember the sincere faith that had first dwelt in his grandmother and his mother. The use of the word "first" indicates that Lois was the first in her family to become a Christian. Having reminisced briefly about Timothy's heritage, Paul ended with his solid and unassailable conviction about the nature of Timothy's personal faith. This affirmation prepared the way for a call to specific action.

Kindle Afresh the Gift (vv. 6-7)

The phrase "for this reason" clearly connects the challenge to "kindle afresh" with Paul's affirmation that Timothy's faith was real and sufficient (v. 6). Timothy did not need any new or extraordinary gift to fulfill his duties in Ephesus; he only needed to "kindle afresh" the gift that was in him. The word translated "kindle afresh" is used only here in the New Testament. The root word refers to rearranging embers in which the flame has diminished. It can mean either "to kindle afresh" or "to keep in full flame." Paul was not suggesting that Timothy had lost his early fire, but he was simply affirming that Christian ministry required that all believers keep their flame at full intensity.

The phrase "gift of God" contains the Greek word *charisma*, which Paul used consistently to speak of supernatural empowering and gifting for ministry. The gifting for ministry is related to the "laying on" of hands, which speaks of the commissioning for a particular task. The laying on of hands was more a recognition of the calling and gifting of an individual than the actual bestowing of a particular gift. Paul used "my" to remind Timothy of his own involvement in this important event.

Paul began verse 7 with a negative, emphasizing that the spirit of timidity is not from God. He may have used the plural "us" to include himself and thus soften the implication that he was criticizing Timothy for personal timidity. In contrast to the one negative is a triad of positives—power, love, and discipline. "Power" refers to the work of the Spirit, enabling the minister to have the strength of character to exercise authority, even when it does not correspond to one's natural inclination. Power devoid of love can be autocratic and destructive. Love without the other two qualities can be sentimentalism. Discipline without the other two can be legalism. It is the combination of the three that enables us to minister without fear.

The Gospel and the Minister (vv. 8-11)

Paul asserted next that Timothy should not allow his natural temperament to lead to shame concerning the testimony about our Lord (1:8; cf. 1 Cor. 1:6). The Christian message as a whole, with its emphasis on the cross, could bring ignominy to those who preached it (cf. 1 Cor. 1:23). Since imprisonment carried with it a certain social stigma, Timothy might be tempted to be ashamed of his mentor's present circumstances.

Paul was so assured of God's purpose and ability to bring about good in every circumstance that he described himself as "His prisoner." Roman authorities might have placed him in jail, but Paul had already become slave and prisoner to the Lord. Paul invited Timothy to join him in suffering for the gospel. The phrase "according to the power of God" reminds us that sharing in suffering for the gospel is never undertaken in our own strength.

The apostle began with twin affirmations that God has *saved* us and *called* us (v. 9). Paul used the word "Savior" six times in the Pastorals, giving prominence to God's saving activity. "Called us with a holy calling" speaks of vocation. Salvation from a life of sin is only one side of salvation. The other is the calling to a life of holiness. Our holy calling is to be set apart for His service no matter our profession.

Our salvation and calling was not accomplished by human effort, but according to God's purpose and grace. Grace, by definition, can never be earned but is given to us in Christ Jesus. The free gift of grace that would reside "in Christ Jesus" was God's plan from all eternity. The idea expressed here is more completely explained in Ephesians 1:3-12. God's eternal purpose was to make every spiritual blessing available "in Christ" before the foundation of the world. For persons to experience these blessings they must listen to the gospel, believe, and be sealed "in Him" by the Spirit (Eph. 1:13). What is determined before creation is not "who" will receive grace but "how" anyone can receive grace.

In verse 10 the thought moves from eternity to time. Grace was clearly revealed through the incarnation of God's Son (cf. John 1:14, 16). His appearing "abolished death." Paul used the same word in 1 Corinthians 15:26 when he spoke of death being the last enemy to be destroyed. In Corinthians Paul was speaking of a future event, whereas here he used aorist verbs to speak of the whole range of Christ's redemptive work as an accomplished fact. Though physical death remains, it no longer possesses sting or victory and thus need not be feared.

Christ not only destroyed death, He "brought life and immortality to light" (v. 10). Both were obscured by the darkness of a sinful world, but the declaration of the gospel flooded them with light. The linking of immortality and life indicates that Christians inherit a life that cannot decay, and thus death cannot destroy the hope we possess in Christ.

The *gospel* means the entire revelation of God in Christ; His life, teaching, death, and resurrection. Having mentioned the glorious gospel, Paul paused to declare in sheer wonder, "for which I was appointed a preacher and an apostle and a teacher" (v. 11; cf. 1 Tim. 2:7). It may be that Paul used all three to assist

Timothy, who was using the apostle's letters and name in defeating the false teachers.

Not Ashamed (v. 12)

Since Paul's imprisonment and suffering was the direct result of his calling as a preacher of the gospel, Timothy had no cause for shame or fear. This bold affirmation of total confidence in God was designed to assist Timothy in his own suffering for the gospel.

We cannot overlook the intensely personal quality of Paul's faith seen in repetition of personal references to God. Paul's use of "whom" rather than "what" underlines the intimate personal relationship between himself and God, which daily had become more vital to the aging warrior. The verbs "believed," "convinced," and "entrusted" indicate a settled conviction that would sustain Paul until the Lord's return ("that day"). Paul had "entrusted" to God his life and ministry, his very soul.

Guard the Treasure (vv. 13-14)

As Timothy stood against the false teachers, he was to hold as a pattern the sound words he had heard from the apostle. Paul used an interesting word from the world of architecture. The "standard" was an outline sketch an architect would use to establish the detailed plans of a building. The content of Timothy's teaching must be consistent with the pattern he had been given. The idea is similar to using a confessional statement such as the Apostle's Creed as a pattern for all of one's teaching and life.

The phrase "in the faith and love" (v. 13) qualifies the act of holding. The manner in which one maintains orthodoxy is as important as the fact of maintaining it. If we follow Paul's advice to Timothy, we would avoid the bitterness and broken relationships that sometime accompany theological discussion and disagreement.

Verse 14 provides further amplification on the command to retain the standard of sound words. "Guard" is the same word used in verse 12 for God guarding the deposit Paul had entrusted to Him. It is now used for the "treasure" that Timothy must keep secure. Although Timothy must exert human effort, he could not achieve this goal unless empowered by the Holy Spirit who indwelled him.

The treasure that must be guarded is the gospel in its largest sense, which includes "the standard of sound words" that Timothy had heard from Paul (cf. 1 Tim. 6:20). It is a treasure because it belongs to God and results in His glory through the salvation of those who through faith accept it. To guard it, Timothy must defend it from attack by the false teachers; he must not allow it to be altered, and he must declare it with boldness.

For Memory and Meditation

"For God has not given us a spirit of timidity, but of power and love and discipline." (2 Tim. 1:7)

---

1 The suggested reconstruction for all the Pastoral Epistles follows closely that of William Hendricksen, *I-II Timothy and Titus* (Grand Rapids, MI: Baker Book House, 1957), 39–43.

Auxano Press Non-Disposable Curriculum

- Designed for use in any small group
- Affordable, biblically based, and life oriented
- Choose your own material and stop and start times
- Study the Bible and build a Christian library

Auxano
PRESS

For teaching guides and additional small group study materials, or to learn about other Auxano Press titles, visit Auxanopress.com.

Other Books by Ken Hemphill

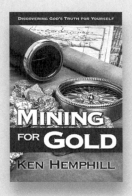

Do you believe God's truth is more precious than gold? Do you dig into God's Word with the same passion you would exert to find physical gold? Learn three different styles of reading and eight essential questions to ask of every text to help you discover the pure riches of God's Word.

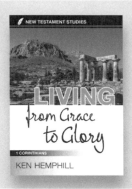

In 1 Corinthians Paul anchors the Christian life in the grace of God, affirming that our eyes, ears, and hearts have not yet comprehended all God has prepared. If you want to know what God has in store for you and your church, study *Living from Grace to Glory* and discover what you have to offer Christ through His church.

For teaching guides and additional small group study materials, or to learn about other Auxano Press titles, visit Auxanopress.com.

More from
Ken Hemphill

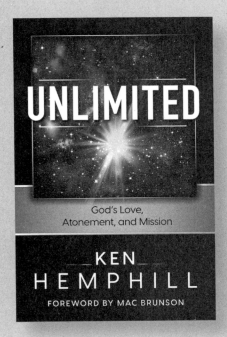

This study of the love, atonement, and mission of God addresses the crucial issue of the extent of the gospel and who can respond to the good news. It will encourage every person to confidently join Unlimited God in His Kingdom mission to redeem the peoples of the whole world.